MY BAT BOY DAYS

Lessons I Learned from the Boys of Summer

Steve Garvey

with Ken Gurnick
and Candace Garvey

SCRIBNER

New York   London   Toronto   Sydney

SCRIBNER

A Division of Simon & Schuster, Inc.
1230 Avenue of the Americas
New York, NY 10020

First Scribner hardcover edition March 2008

SCRIBNER and design are trademarks of
The Gale Group, Inc., used under license
by Simon & Schuster, the publisher of this work.

For information about special discounts for bulk purchases,
please contact Simon & Schuster Special Sales:
1-800-456-6798 or business@simonandschuster.com

Text set in Scala

Manufactured in the United States of America

1   3   5   7   9   10   8   6   4   2

Library of Congress Cataloging-in-Publication Data
Garvey, Steve, 1948–
My bat boy days : lessons I learned from the boys of summer /
Steve Garvey.—1st Scribner hardcover ed.
p.   cm.
1. Garvey, Steve, 1948– 2. Baseball players—United States—Biography.
I. Title.
GV865.A1G367 2008
796.357092—dc22   2007052351
[B]

ISBN-13: 978-1-4165-4825-6

Baseball bat image on p. iii courtesy of Hillerich & Bradsby Co.

To my children,

May you read this book and hopefully understand why Dad is who he is and never stop dreaming and believing in God. He is always with you and dreams really do come true.

All my love,
Dad

And to my first grandson,
Oliver.
Grandpa loves you.

CONTENTS

MY BAT BOY DAYS

PROLOGUE

Do you believe in destiny?

Some lives are planned and others amount to a series of circumstances, but mine feels like destiny. It started with my grandfather, a Brooklyn policeman, who had the beat of Ebbets Field, listening to the crowd cheer on the Bums from the outside and loving every minute of it. My grandfather, Joseph Patrick Garvey, never did see a game inside the ballpark. That's how my journey, my family's journey, begins.

Early in 1948 my mother's father, Joe Winkler, decided he had enough of the gas station business and the cold winters of Long Island, New York. He sold the property and purchased a motel in Tampa, Florida. He called my parents and convinced them that a warm climate and a new career were ahead, and they packed their belongings and migrated to Florida. My father, Joe Garvey, had served in the navy during World War II and had tried different occupations in pursuit of his ultimate career. Mildred Garvey had worked for American Airlines and was pregnant with me when they joined my grandparents on the trip down South.

The motel, unfortunately, was over a mile from Highway 301, the main route between west Florida and the northeastern seaboard, and as we have learned, business is usually about location and convenience, neither of which the motel possessed. The property struggled, but on December 22, 1948, I was born, at about seven and half pounds with a full set of lungs. My dad said, "Steve looks like a lot of work," so needless to say I was an only child. By early 1950 the motel had become a losing venture and was sold. Both my parents and grandparents decided to stay and make Florida their permanent residence. My dad began working as a city transit bus driver and my mother's secretarial skills were put to use.

By 1955 the Garvey family was deeply rooted in Tampa soil, my mother working for Continental Insurance and my dad driving for Greyhound. Dad chose to work the "extra board" instead of a set route for more flexibility in his schedule. He frequently had charters with groups going to sporting events, or with sports teams, and for a former football and baseball player this was the fun part of the job. That fall I entered the second grade and by the end of September had become very interested in the baseball World Series. My mother was a Yankees fan and my father a Dodgers fan, so you can imagine there was a steady banter between two New Yorkers who loved their teams. Because my dad's father was a Brooklyn policeman, I cheered mostly for the Bums. I still loved to watch Mickey Mantle and Yogi Berra hit and play the game, but by the ninth inning of game seven the Dodgers were clearly my favorite.

The World Series in 1955 was played in daylight and aired in black and white on television across America. For those of us going to school on the East Coast, by three o'clock, it was already about the seventh inning. After school, I would hop on my bike and ride as fast as I could for over a mile. Most days I would rush into the house and catch the last two innings. Pitchers' duels were dreaded, and lots of offense was prayed for. I clearly remember Don Larsen's perfect game a few years later, when I burst through the door to see the last two pitches against Dale Mitchell to end the game. Unfortunately, today's programming makes it almost impossible for a kid to stay up for the last two innings of any game, even a historic no-hitter. My growing infatuation with the game, along with the knowledge that my dad and a few other fathers were starting a Little League in our Drew Park neighborhood, provided the foundation for my interest in playing baseball, this sport that my parents loved. At the age of seven, I was just beginning to experience the joys of our national pastime. By March of '56, I was playing catch and entertaining myself by playing stickball games, dragging kids out of their homes to play games that ended up being the Dodgers against the Yankees. Sometimes I was "the Mick," but usually I was one of the Bums. Those were the good ole days! Somehow, some way, the Brooklyn Dodgers always came back in the ninth inning of game seven and won the World Series, and always against the Yankees.

ON THE BUS

It was the spring of 1956. Dwight D. Eisenhower was president of the United States, a new fast-food franchise called McDonald's sold twenty-five-cent hamburgers, Milton Berle and Red Skelton dominated the airwaves, black-and-white television was America's new form of must-have technology, and most important, the Brooklyn Dodgers were the World Champions of baseball, having beaten the New York Yankees in the 1955 World Series.

I was a young boy in a transplanted family from Long Island, New York, developing roots in the Tampa, Florida, area, with two hardworking parents. The evening of March 28, 1956, was typical for the Garvey family. My father and mother would try to be home most evenings at five for family dinners, and this evening was no different. As we sat down to fried chicken, mashed potatoes, and peas, a meal I will never forget, my dad asked me the usual question:

"Steve, how was your day, son, did you learn anything new?"

As usual, I answered, good, no, and can I get up and go out and play? Then the unusual, life-changing, dream-beginning question:

"Do you have any test tomorrow, and if you don't, do you want to skip school?"

Now, I had never heard those questions before and a quick look to Mom's smiling face meant something special was about to happen.

"I have a charter tomorrow to pick up the Brooklyn Dodgers at the Tampa airport and take them to Al Lang Field in St. Petersburg. The Yankees are playing the Dodgers and I thought it might be a great father-and-son day for us."

For a young boy who was about to start his first Little League season, this was an exciting moment, filled with questions and a quick trip to my Hav-a-Tampa Cigar box, busting with baseball cards. I spent what seemed like hours looking for all my favorite Dodgers so I could go over stats with the guys on the bus. I called my grandfather in New York, a Brooklyn police officer, and asked who his favorite Dodgers were. Pee Wee, Carl, and the

Duke, he said. And how he loved Carl Furillo, the ultimate blue-collar everyday player.

Morning came and I woke up and put on my blue jeans
and Ban-Lon shirt. Ban-Lon shirts were the polo shirts of
the fifties and came in thirteen colors. This one was a
royal blue, almost like Dodger blue. With a little butch
wax to keep my flattop sticking up, I was ready to go at
6:00 A.M.

By seven we had picked up the new scenic-cruiser
from the Greyhound bus station and were on our way to
Tampa International Airport. Dad emphasized the need
to be respectful, to not get in the way, and most important, to say "yes sir" and "no sir." I listened carefully,
knowing full well that I was awestruck even before I actually saw these great men. By eight-fifteen, we were standing on the tarmac waiting for the Dodger airplane, the
Kay O'Malley 1, named after the wife of the owner, Walter O'Malley. The plane hit the runway, and within a
minute it had thundered and decelerated by us. I will
never forget the Dodger logo written across the body of
the plane and a white baseball with red stitches on the
tail. The DC 7 taxied to within thirty yards of the bus, and

with no Jetways to greet the planes in those days, a stairway was pushed to the open door, and the men began to board the bus. My dad told me to stand near the door, but "Don't block it," so I could see these great Dodgers close up. Off came the skipper, Walter Alston, who was working on the fourth of twenty-two one-year contracts and a Hall of Fame career. He was followed by Pee Wee Reese, Jim Gilliam, Carl Erskine, Duke Snider, and on and on. As each man passed by me, he would pat me on the head. I don't know whether they did this as an endearing gesture, or if they just wanted to feel my proudly waxed flattop. Finally, the last two players approached. One of them was Roy Campanella, the MVP catcher. The other could only be Jackie Robinson, who was constantly center stage during the '55 World Series and was probably the most significant player in baseball history. This was major to a boy from the South. Even at my age, I knew history was standing before me, and it was much bigger than baseball.

Roy and Jackie asked me if I played baseball. I said I would be starting Little League in a week. At least I think that's what came out. When you are as nervous as I was, sometimes air is all that comes out. Roy said, "If you practice hard and listen to your coaches, maybe someday you'll be a Dodger." I nodded, and then Roy asked me if I was doing well in school. That threw me, because the truth was I had been having a tough time. My dad was standing close by and jumped in with, "Roy, Stevie's struggling with reading, but we're working hard each night and he's trying hard." My dad was wearing a name tag with a Greyhound dog on top, and Roy responded, "Joe, if Steve studies hard and practices, maybe someday he'll be a Dodger!" Dad and I looked at each other and smiled, while Jackie and Roy both, you guessed it, patted me on the head and walked onto the bus. I only grew to be five foot ten, but my dad was six foot three, so part of me wonders if all that patting on the head didn't stunt my growth!

The drive from the airport to Al Lang field in St. Pete was about forty minutes. I stood in the stairwell one step from Dad, who was behind the wheel. I held on to the guardrail and glanced at the men on the bus. Walter Alston and another coach sat in the front row and most of the players were talking or reading papers. I would learn years later that the manager always gets the first seat on the left—as a sign of respect, I believe, and to give the players a chance to do their talking behind him. We finally pulled into the Al Lang parking lot and maneuvered to a space in front of the visiting clubhouse. Dad opened the compartments under the bus, and each player, coach, and manager grabbed his equipment bags and headed for the clubhouse. A man suddenly emerged from the clubhouse, dressed in boxer shorts and a strapped T-shirt, with a little cigar wedged into the side of his mouth. We would later find out that he was John Griffin, the equipment manager and a throwback to a different time. "Buddy," the man said, "does the kid want to be a bat boy?" "Sure!" my dad said. "Well, let's get the bats, balls, and catchers' bags to the dugout, set out the helmets, and put the towels on the bench." Each bag weighed more than anything I had ever lifted, but Dad helped me and we got all the equipment ready for batting practice.

The first player to come out was Gil Hodges. When I saw him in street clothes, he seemed to be about my dad's size, but now in the Dodger gray wool uniform he looked much bigger. He picked up a ball and motioned as if he wanted to play catch with me. Me! I pointed my finger at myself, he nodded, and I grabbed my new Rawlings mitt. His first toss was arced high and intended to test my ability. I must have impressed him with a clean catch, as the next few throws were harder. I remember feeling a sting with each one and wondering if the new gear had enough padding. More and more players came out, and finally Gil said, "One more, son!" That last toss had no spin to it and only my chest kept it from going by me. The loud thud probably scared Mr. Hodges, who came up to me to see if I was all right. The pitch had knocked the wind out of me a little bit, but I gave him an "okay" nod—mainly because I couldn't speak! Just then, the Yankees ended pregame batting practice, and the Dodgers took the field for fifty minutes of hitting, fielding, and stretching.

Now all the players looked bigger—not just Hodges, but Furillo, Snider, Robinson, Campanella, and even Reese. Maybe it was the wool uniform itself or the cleated shoes that added height. These men were World Champions, baseball stars from the largest market in the country. They had suddenly walked off the baseball cards I had in my pocket and come to life. What I noticed over the next hour was how smoothly and effortlessly these players used their skills. Everyone seemed to have a routine that prepared him for the game. I still had not played my first game in Little League, but by watching and listening I was learning more about the game than I ever could have on my own. I have learned that we human beings are great imitators. What we see over and over again, we frequently can absorb and embody.

Practice ended and the cleanup began. Pads were picked up, bats placed in the rack, and helmets put in a special case. A gooey rag and a powdery sack were placed on the first steps of the dugout. The rag had liquid pine tar on it that hitters used for a better grip on their bats, and the bag was rosin, which the pitchers used to keep their hands dry. Hitters also used the rosin on their bats, and combined with the tar, it formed a glue that would prevent any grip from slipping. I picked up a new ball made from horsehide, stitched in twine, and with a smell like nothing else. This pure white ball, nine inches around, weighing five ounces, and with 108 stitches, was like a diamond to me. When no one was looking, I tried on Pee Wee's shortstop mitt and Campy's catcher's mitt. The cowhide felt much softer than my mitt. I wondered if they had used them in the championship last fall. Finally, I picked up a couple of Louisville sluggers, heavy for a seven-year-old, but it was still a thrill to hold a lathed piece of wood that is used to perform the toughest act in sports, hitting a baseball.

I put everything in its place and walked back to the clubhouse. Dad gave me a turkey sandwich and a cola, but I barely touched either. It was time for the game, and I actually felt like a Dodger with a job to do.

I honestly don't remember much about the game. I know the Dodgers won, and I think most of the players appeared in the game. The Yankees had an awe-inspiring aura about them. They seemed even bigger than the Dodgers. While the 1955 World Championship was the Dodgers' first, the Yankees had sixteen and were considered the greatest franchise in the game. Each player was a potential All-Star, and the power of the New York press inflated the notoriety of even the most average of players.

When the game was over, the traveling secretary, Lee Scott, shouted, "Bus leaves in thirty minutes." That meant no fooling around, and I had to quickly get the gear packed and on the bus. Dad helped me carry the heavy bat bag. The helmet case was bulky but manageable. I cleaned up the dugout, just as I would my room at home. A few minutes later most of the team was on the bus, and Dad was closing the doors to the storage compartments. I got a tap on the shoulder and there stood John the "clubhouse man."

"Good job, kid," he said. "These are for you." He handed me two autographed balls and a couple of brand-new ones. My response was a simple "Thank-you," and I stuffed two in each pocket—easy to do when you are wearing "husky" size jeans.

Within the hour, our bus pulled onto the tarmac of Tampa International Airport and there waiting for the team was the *Kay O'Malley 1*. The players and management filed off the bus and onto the plane. Some said good-bye, others were still eating the last of the sandwiches for the day. Lee Scott shook Dad's hand and said he would see him soon. Dad looked down and saw a fifty-dollar bill in his big hand, easily the biggest tip of his career at Greyhound. Dad and I stood in front of the bus, his arm around my shoulder, as the plane taxied down the runway and finally took off into the beautiful pink and gray Florida sunset. My dad asked me what I thought of the day, and I looked at him and said, "Dad, this was the greatest day of my life." All seven years of it.

We walked to the door of the bus and Dad said, "Why don't you sit in the manager's seat?" I remember thinking I'd never forget who gets to sit in seat 1A. As I started to sit down, I saw two used bats, broken at the handle. I looked at Dad, and he said, "I thought you might like these." They were game-used by Duke Snider and Carl Furillo, given to my dad by the clubhouse man after I had gotten on the bus at Al Lang Field. As I ran my hand down the bat and gripped the handle, my dad told me to be careful of splinters. I probably thought, as young boys do, that just one little one might not hurt. Kind of a souvenir of the day with the Dodgers. All the way to the bus station we talked about the day. The players, the game, what a neat plane they had, and the stuff we were going to tell Mom at dinner.

Around six-thirty we came bounding through the door of our house, me calling for Mom and Dad bidding, "Hi, Mill." Mom came around the corner of the kitchen, gave us big hugs, and offered several "Ohs" and "Ahs" over the bats and balls. It was a special moment in our lives—just the beginning of a new direction for the Garvey family.

Dinner was longer than usual. I didn't just say yes, no, or can I be excused. Instead, I told story after story from that day. I used words I had never used. But more important, my mother and father could sense the enthusiasm I had for baseball and these great players. Finally, I ran out of steam.

I went into my room and showered quickly, too quickly, and put on my pajamas. I pulled down the covers and jumped into bed. I thought I would fall fast asleep, but I smelled a strong odor. My dad stuck his head into the room, as parents do when checking on their supposed-to-be-sleeping children, and whispered, "Are you sleeping?" I think he was startled when I said, "No!" He came over to my bed and asked me what was wrong. I said that I was tired, but there was a smell keeping me awake. He came over and sniffed around. He pulled back and smiled.

"Did you wash your hands?" he asked. I was slow to answer, so he said, "You know that sticky stuff the players used on their bats?"

"Pine tar," I replied.

"Yes," he said, "that's what you're smelling."

I expected him to order me back to the bathroom, but instead he casually said, "Son, you will probably never forget that smell for the rest of your life!"

After my bat boy baptism in 1956, for six ensuing years the Dodgers would request my dad to drive them when they came to the Tampa Bay area. The Greyhound dispatchers who assigned these charters would also give Dad an occasional Yankees, Tigers, or Reds trip, knowing that he loved those "baseball days" and understood the teams' requirements. I would always join Dad for the

Dodgers, even skipping school during a weekday, and if the other trips fell on the weekend I would be there. Dad always told the clubhouse manager for a given team that I had been a bat boy for other teams and would do a good job. I learned that each team was different in personality, attitude, and approach to the game. Not every team was as organized and structured as the Dodgers. Sure, spring training was just a warm-up for the regular season, but the Dodger history and pride had shown through even during the meaningless games. When the score was close, that desire to win anywhere, any time made the difference. It was one of the greatest lessons I learned.

My story, of course, doesn't end after six years as a bat boy. Those years simply laid the foundation for a lifetime love affair with our national pastime. Most of you will know that I had a wonderful and blessed career with the same Dodger organization I grew up with, and I spent the last five years of my career with the San Diego Padres. Several people whom I met as a bat boy were still with the organization in 1968 when I was selected in the first round of the secondary phase of the draft. To have run errands for manager Walt Alston and then to have played for him; to see traveling secretary Lee Scott give

my dad a tip and then to ask Scotty for twenty-two tick-
ets on my first visit to Shea Stadium; to see Campy, Pee
Wee, and Carl Erskine around the organization as I
became a veteran Dodger, well . . . it was a dream come
true, there's no doubt.

Do experiences like the ones I had as a young boy lead
to success? Or is it a coincidence? Can you learn enough
from watching and listening to your heroes to make
yourself into a player just like them? Do you have to have
God-given skills, or can hard work and dedication make
the difference? I'm not sure of the answers, but I suspect
my career in baseball was, at the very least, tremendously enhanced by my bat boy days.

I was given an incredible opportunity to learn from
this wonderful group of ballplayers, the Boys of Summer, as author Roger Kahn referred to the Brooklyn
Dodgers of the 1950s in his seminal book. What I
learned from this last great generation of men who
played baseball has served me to this day and can provide a blueprint for anyone with a dream and the determination to make it come true.

The many lessons learned have been the keys to my
own success in baseball and in life. The journey started
that day on my father's bus, surrounded by these giant

men who were like immortals to me. To have had the God-given talent to play the great game of baseball at the ultimate level, and to have learned from the men who were the soul of the game, has been a blessing. I have written this book to honor my heroes. They taught me about the game and how it should be played and lived. Those lessons were learned years ago, but they are timeless.

THE LEADERSHIP
OF PEE WEE REESE

Among the many ways that baseball has changed over the years is the gradual disappearance of the team captain. The 1956 Dodgers had the best, Pee Wee Reese. Back then, most captains of baseball teams were shortstops or catchers. Reese fit the profile as the heart of the defense and catalyst of the offense. That first day as a bat boy, I noticed that the players would refer to one another by their first or last names or by nicknames. But everybody called Reese "Cap." I remember when Reese saw the Yankees on the field that day, he was quick with the barbs left over from the previous fall's World Series. Journalists followed Reese everywhere that day. Pee Wee was always good for a colorful story or quotation.

As a ballplayer, Reese was the greatest on-field manager I ever saw. He would, for example, move an outfielder to the right spot based on a given hitter's tendency, a duty now handled by the coaching staff from the dugout. But Reese didn't need such coaching. If Mickey Mantle was batting left-handed, Cap would subtly signal Duke Snider to shade to right-center field. I once saw him settle down a nervous rookie pitcher, who struck out the next two batters. That's leadership. Cap was a leader even to a new bat boy like me. He told me the key to baseball, whether you're batting or fielding, is to never, ever take your eye off the ball from the moment it leaves the pitcher's mitt. Sounds simple, but it's sage advice for a kid learning the game.

Pee Wee Reese was elected into baseball's Hall of Fame by the Veterans Committee in 1984. He was a ten-time All-Star shortstop and career-long Dodger, whose first major league season was 1940 in Brooklyn and whose last was 1958, the Dodgers' first year in Los Angeles. His best offensive season was 1954, when he hit .309 with 69 RBIs and 98 runs scored, although he led the league with 132 runs scored in 1949.

At age twelve, Pee Wee was a ranking marble shooter. That—and not his size—is how he got his nickname. The Pee Wee is the shooting marble. He played basketball as well as baseball in high school and after graduating went to work for the phone company as a cable splicer, earning $18 a week. He starred at shortstop for his church baseball league and was signed for $200 by the local Louisville Colonels, a team soon purchased for $195,000 by the Boston Red Sox. When the Sox needed a replacement for shortstop Joe Cronin, Reese was considered a likely candidate. When asked his opinion, however, Cronin was not impressed with Reese, and the Red Sox moved him to the Dodgers that same spring. Larry MacPhail paid $40,000 cash and four players to get him. As part of the deal, Reese received $3,750 of the cash.

Considered an ideal replacement at shortstop for the aging Leo Durocher, Reese made his major league debut for Brooklyn in 1940 and became an everyday player in 1941, but missed three seasons (1943–45) serving in the navy during World War II. For a fascinating *Sport* magazine essay in 1951, Milton Gross spoke with Reese's management and teammates to determine exactly when and how Reese transformed from a young player into a veteran leader, who, general manager Branch Rickey believed, might eventually succeed manager Burt Shotton.

Reese suggested the turning point might have been a 1950 game at Wrigley Field against the Cubs that not only marked Reese's one thousandth major league game, but was the first one from which he was ejected. The Dodgers led, 9–0, when Reese was called out on strikes on a 3-2 pitch by plate umpire Babe Pinelli. According to Gross, Reese said nothing, but turned furiously, glared at the umpire, and tossed his bat over his head. Pinelli ejected Reese, who returned to the dugout as coach Clyde Sukeforth was about to argue with Pinelli, but Reese stopped him.

"Let it be," Reese said to Sukeforth. "It's the first time. Maybe it makes me a man."

Durocher disagreed and said Reese demonstrated leadership skills to him much sooner, specifically in a 1946 exhibition game at Daytona Beach after returning from the navy. Reese made the hardest play there is for a shortstop, ranging quickly into the hole between shortstop and third base, backhanding a sharp grounder, planting, and firing an off-balance throw to beat the runner at first base.

"When the inning was over, Reese trotted back to the dugout," said Durocher. "I looked at him for a minute. There was that little kid's grin that I remembered when he went off to the service after the 1942 season, still on his face. But I knew this wasn't a kid any more. I gave him the wink and he gave it back to me. I said to him, 'You went away to war a boy and you came back a man.' "

It would be three more years before Reese was appointed captain of the Dodgers by Rickey. The title came with an extra $500 salary, the daily assignment of taking the lineup card to home plate, and the difficult task of serving as a liaison between the players and management. When Gross asked Rickey why Reese wasn't named captain until 1949, Rickey told the reporter to seek out Jackie Robinson for the best answer.

"I'll talk to you about that fellow for an hour, or a day, or a year," Robinson said of Reese. "Everybody respects and follows that fellow. In my book, there's none finer. A really nice man is a rare thing. The crowd always spots him. They guessed right about Pee Wee. I could tell them a lot more."

Robinson explained that Reese, having been reared on a small tobacco and corn farm in rural Kentucky, came from a world where racial prejudice was commonplace. Reese's family, of Dutch-Irish extraction, moved from little Ekron to Louisville so Reese's father could earn a regular salary as a detective for the Louisville and Nashville Railroad. Reese, though, told the story of how he heard that the Dodgers had signed the first Negro to be admitted to major league baseball. Reese was on a navy ship bringing him home from Guam and a shipmate showed him a news item about Robinson's signing and wanted to know what Pee Wee thought about it. Reese asked what position this Robinson played and was told shortstop.

"Just my luck," Reese said. "Another guy to fight for my job."

Reese later said his reaction was an intentional deflection from the racial overtones of the question, a necessary diversion, because he wasn't sure about his answer. He knew if Rickey signed the player, it was because he thought Robinson could help the Dodgers. But Reese admitted he immediately thought about the possible personal fallout. When they finally became teammates, Reese realized the pressure that Robinson was under, how opponents would try harder against him and fans would hurl brutal comments at him from the stands. Reese knew Robinson played with the pressure of knowing that if he failed, his race might never get another chance to play Major League Baseball. Reese wondered how he would have held up to that kind of pressure.

"I was brought up in Louisville," Reese once told Roger Kahn, author of *The Boys of Summer*. "I grew up in a neighborhood where they didn't think too much of colored people. It affected me. Where you grow up has to. The first thing I thought about when I heard about Jackie being signed was why does it have to be a shortstop, why does he have to be playing my position, why does he have to be after my job? Then I thought what would the people around Louisville think? I thought for a real long time and pretty soon I was trying to put myself in Robinson's position.

"'Suppose the colored league was the big league,' I figured. 'Suppose I was the first white guy to play in that league. What would it be like for me?' Well, I knew what it would be like. It would be rugged as hell. So I tried to put myself in Jack's position. That helped. It helped me to understand him and to have respect for what he was trying to do. He did this amazing thing, this unbelievable thing, when you know him, and he deserves all the credit in the world."

Robinson saw it differently. "He did so many things to help me," he said of Reese. "So many for which I'll be eternally grateful to him."

Robinson recalled several occasions where Reese went out of his way to include Robinson in off-the-field activities like a round of golf, but he also recalled the time the

Montreal Royals went to Macon, Georgia, presenting Robinson with the opportunity to be the first African American to play in a game with whites in that city. The Ku Klux Klan pointed to the game as an illustration of the anticipated weakening of segregation laws in the South. When the Dodgers arrived in Macon, Robinson received a death threat letter.

In pregame warm-ups, Reese noticed Robinson playing catch alongside him. "Get away from me, you human target," Reese joked. "That guy will take a shot at you, miss, and hit me. I don't look good with holes in me."

Said Robinson: "I had been tied up in scared little knots, but when Pee Wee gave me that rib everything kind of loosened inside me. That's the way it's been all year and that's the way it's been ever since."

Reese was once ordered by the fiery manager Durocher to become the holler guy of the team.

"You're another me," Durocher said to Reese. "Run this team on the field the way I would run it if I were out there."

But Reese was just a kid surrounded by veterans like Dolf Camilli and Cookie Lavagetto. Rickey explained the reason he waited until well into Reese's career to make him captain was the departures of all of Reese's heroes.

"You are the logical one to hold our team together," Rickey told Reese. "It is not only I who respect you, your ability, and your judgment, it is the other boys as well."

Reese led with words, but also by example. One of his traits that I can especially relate to is the desire to play every day, even when hurt. In his first season with the Dodgers, Reese was beaned by Cubs pitcher Jake Mooty and spent eighteen days in the hospital, but never showed any effects at bat. He played part of that season with a broken bone in his heel. In 1946, he was taken out at second base on a hard slide and landed on the back of his neck. He stayed in the game, but when severe pain lingered, he was diagnosed with a chipped vertebra and fitted for a brace manufactured for people with broken necks. He missed two games. He played the 1948 season with a hernia that required winter surgery.

Had Rickey not parted ways with new owner Walter O'Malley and left for Pittsburgh, he probably would have chosen Reese to succeed Shotton. But O'Malley explained that there was too much at stake in his first year as Rickey's successor to name a first-year manager, so he went with veteran Chuck Dressen. Reese was never officially approached for the job at the time.

But two years later, when Dressen demanded a multiyear contract, he wound up with none at all. Here's how Reese described the situation to *Baseball Digest* in 1954.

"When Dressen left the Dodgers, I was mentioned prominently for the job," he wrote. "They sounded me out and I guess I could have had it, if I wanted it. I finally told them no. I said the same thing I had said three years before when I was being mentioned as a possible successor to Shotton. Playing is a full-time job. So is managing. You can't do a good job at either if you try to do both. And I feel I've got two or three more years at shortstop."

Duke Snider, in his autobiography, *The Duke of Flatbush*, described what Reese meant to the Dodgers.

"Knowing Pee Wee Reese and playing on the same team with him have been two of the blessings in my life," wrote Snider. "Reese was our captain, and to this day, 40 years after those magical times began, we still address him by that title. He was our unquestioned leader. He led by his example, making so many big plays and getting so many big hits over his 16 years in the Majors, all of them with the Dodgers. Without Pee Wee, we wouldn't have won as many pennants as we did. And when we finally won our first World Series, beating the Yankees in 1955, it was only right that the last out of the Series, a ground ball by Elston Howard, was hit to Pee Wee.

"Pee Wee was our leader in other ways, too. He helped me tremendously with the mental approach to the game. So much of baseball is the mental alertness and anticipation to make the right play. And you had to sustain that level of mental sharpness over a season of 154 games. That's not easy even if you have the physical tools, and that's why Pee Wee was so important to the Dodgers as a team and to so many of us individually. That's why we called him 'Captain,' and why there was a captain's chair, one with arms, in front of his locker, while the rest of us sat on stools."

I've heard it said that 98 percent of people are followers and 2 percent are leaders. True leaders possess an uncanny sense of what needs to be done, at the right time and in the right place. Pee Wee seemed to always be in that place at the time. He was vocal when he had to be and led by example when that was the right choice. The Dodgers would quickly learn it wasn't his glove, or bat, not even his judgment on the field, that made him so valuable. They made him the "Captain" because of his ability to lead the Boys of Summer like no other ever had and no one ever would again.

THE DIGNITY
OF GIL HODGES

As I was putting the bats in order before that 1956 spring-training game between the Dodgers and Yankees, straightening out the helmets and throwing the rosin bag and pine tar into the on-deck circle, it was Gil Hodges, six foot four, with massive hands and a gentle-giant demeanor, who offered to play catch with me, gradually showing me the mechanics of throwing and catching. Hodges was the first to teach me lessons about digging balls out of the dirt and the smooth footwork around the first-base bag that would put me years ahead of the other kids. Over the next several years, Gil always had ten minutes to share with a bat boy. He would go on to win three Gold Gloves and, maybe not coincidentally, I would win four. No ballpark could contain his powerful swing, and crucial home runs were his trademark. Brooklynites loved their favorite son, and when he struggled through a disastrous 0-for-21 batting slump in the 1952 World Series, Catholic churches throughout the borough had parishioners saying novenas for Number 14. He brought dignity to Da Bums of Brooklyn.

This is why *Sport* magazine, in a 1957 profile by Bill Roeder, called Hodges "The Dodger Who's Never Been Booed." When Hodges's slump from that 1952 World Series continued for three weeks into the 1953 regular season, Brooklyn fans faithfully supported him. And when he finally hit his first home run that year, there was no sarcastic Bronx cheer but a standing ovation.

Father Herbert Redmond of St. Francis Roman Catholic Church in Brooklyn told his parishioners: "It's far too hot for a homily. Keep the Commandments and say a prayer for Gil Hodges."

Hodges, the son of a coal miner, always seemed to be overshadowed by brighter Dodger stars—Jackie Robinson, Duke Snider, Roy Campanella, Pee Wee Reese. They all wound up in the Hall of Fame, but Hodges never did. Yet in Brooklyn, none of the others was as popular as Hodges. One contributing factor is that he became a year-round Brooklynite. He was from Indiana but married Joan Lombardi from Brooklyn, and they bought a house in Flatbush and reared three children there. During the winter, Gil sold cars at a Brooklyn dealership. At a time when the flight to the suburbs began to affect Brooklyn, Hodges stayed at home. But not necessarily in his home. He circulated in the community, dining and shopping and running errands. He was visible. He was accessible.

And he was willing to help promote the Dodgers. The club had an official named Jim Murray who helped arrange public appearances, and he told Roeder that Hodges couldn't accommodate one-tenth of the requests.

"He's number one on our list," said Murray. "Everywhere I go it's, 'Can we get Gil out? Can we get Gil?' He's kind of a quiet fellow, not an orator, but when they start asking questions he becomes one of the most graceful and comfortable conversationalists you'd ever want to hear. He's kind and gentle and no matter how embarrassing the question he has a knack of turning it into a gem."

Hodges was respectful and cooperative with the media, as well as with umpires, which is why he said he was never ejected from a game. Manager Chuck Dressen, believing Hodges would benefit from showing a little fire at an umpire, offered his first baseman a financial inducement for a game-stopping argument. When Hodges finally confronted an umpire, albeit in a diplomatically stern manner, Dressen shook his hand when he returned to the dugout and slipped him a ten-dollar bill. Hodges slipped it right back into the manager's hand.

"I suppose arguing should be done," said Hodges. "It won't change many decisions, if any, but maybe it does keep umpires on their toes. Still, if you're not built that way it's tough to make yourself get on them, and I guess I'm not built that way."

When club president Branch Rickey sold his stock and father and son moved on to the Pirates, here's how much the younger Rickey, then farm director, thought of Hodges:

"I just don't like to think I'm leaving a club which has Hodges on it. He is everything you look for in a ballplayer, on and off the field."

By that time, Hodges was a star. But the younger Rickey was taken with Hodges long before that. Bird-dog scout Stan Freezie discovered Hodges and brought the future slugger to a 1943 tryout camp attended by the younger Rickey.

"In these tryout camps you see a lot of kids who can run like the dickens and who can throw hard, but it's a rare thing to find a kid who can shillelagh a ball," the son of the club president told Herb Goren in a 1951 interview for *Baseball Digest*. "He just beat the ball to death. I saw him and I said: 'Hornsby or Foxx.' That's what I said."

Hodges, then a nineteen-year-old student at St. Joseph's University in Indiana, signed for a $1,000 bonus and went straight to the Dodgers, mainly because major league rosters had been thinned by World War II. A third baseman and four-sport star in school, Hodges was moved to catcher by Rickey Sr., but after spending the last three months of that season on the Brooklyn bench, he joined the marines and spent two and a half years in the service, including a battle on Okinawa, earning a Bronze Star for bravery.

When Hodges returned from the war, he resumed his baseball career as a catcher, but by 1948, with Roy Campanella destined to be the backstop for a decade, Dodgers manager Leo Durocher made Hodges a first baseman and that's where he stayed, his six-two, two-hundred-pound frame and ten-foot wingspan providing a comforting target for infield throws. He went on to win three Gold Glove Awards and would have had more if they had invented the award sooner.

Of course, it was Hodges's bat that made him a fixture.

In 1950 against Boston, Hodges hit four home runs in one game, and no Dodger would do that again until Shawn Green did fifty-two years later. The next year, Hodges set a Brooklyn single-season record with 40 home runs. He set a record again with 42 in 1954. He drove in more than 100 runs seven consecutive seasons and was an eight-time All-Star. His 370 career home runs were a National League record for right-handed hitters at the time.

In what became a trait among Dodgers first basemen, he didn't miss many games, averaging 152 games from 1949 to 1957, when the season was only 154 games long. He came to Los Angeles with the Dodgers and was a key contributor in their 1959 championship season with 25 homers and 80 RBIs. His eighth-inning homer gave the Dodgers a 5–4 win in game four of the World Series, which the Dodgers went on to win over the White Sox.

After the 1961 season, Hodges was left unprotected by the Dodgers and was selected in the expansion draft by the New York Mets. He played fifty-four games for the Mets in 1962 and after eleven games in 1963 was traded to the Washington Senators for Jimmy Piersall. Hodges was to have been a player/manager for the Senators, but instead announced his retirement as a player to focus on managing. He managed Washington through the 1967 season without a winning season, then returned to New York to manage the "Miracle Mets" to the 1969 World Series Championship over Baltimore, after which he was named Manager of the Year by *The Sporting News*.

Two days short of his forty-eighth birthday, on Easter Sunday 1972, while concluding a day of golf in Palm Beach Lakes with members of his coaching staff during spring training, Hodges suffered a massive heart attack and died.

For more than thirty years, Hodges has been known as the greatest player not in the Hall of Fame. He failed to receive enough votes from baseball writers for fifteen years, even though he received more votes than at least four and as many as ten players who would ultimately be so honored.

"Gil Hodges is a Hall of Fame man," said Jackie Robinson.

My dad has always been my number one hero. He has been my mentor, confidant, and teacher (and occasionally a stern disciplinarian when necessary). He has always respected others and maintained a warmth that has made him likable to everyone. Simply put, Gil Hodges reminded me of my dad. And to think that on my first day as a bat boy, Gil was the first player to spend time with me. For thousands of Greyhound passengers and millions of fans, these two men possessed a quiet dignity that I will always be honored to have learned from.

THE HONESTY
OF CARL ERSKINE

Carl Erskine could have been a judge, arbitrator, senator, or commissioner of baseball, and he would have been great in any of those roles. He exuded honesty. The Anderson, Indiana, native was the most consistent starter and the go-to guy when the Boys of Summer needed a big victory. He was equally important as a team representative, delivering candid answers to tough questions that affected a player's future. He would frequently play devil's advocate to decisions that seemed simple to others, like voting on World Series shares. That might not sound very important if you've never done it, but it's a hot issue when a team divides a pot of bonus money. Carl made it work for the Boys of Summer.

He was the ultimate mediator, and I remember some of the best stories that prove it. Pee Wee Reese was a southerner from Kentucky, and he opened a bowling alley there—a segregated bowling alley, as they all were down there at the time. Now, Pee Wee probably did more to make Jackie Robinson feel welcome when he arrived with the Dodgers than any other player and considered Jackie an equal teammate in every way, but when Jackie learned that Pee Wee owned a segregated bowling alley, it hurt him badly. Robinson never said a word to Pee Wee; that wasn't his style. So Erskine did, because he knew how it hurt Robinson and he knew that for the good of the team this friction needed to be eliminated. Erskine explained the situation to Reese, and Reese sold the bowling alley.

On a Dodgers club that was split over accepting Robinson, Erskine was solidly on Robinson's side. Erskine gave a clue why embracing Robinson was never a problem for him while speaking with author Roger Kahn for *The Boys of Summer*. Erskine remembers his dad taking him to the site of a lynching of two black prisoners outside a nearby jail. Then Erskine told how he had befriended a black boy in grade school.

"Jumpin' Johnny Wilson ate maybe as many meals at my home as he did in his own," Erskine told Kahn. "With a background like that, the Robinson experience simply was no problem. It was really beautiful in a way. Somewhere Jack said he appreciated help from some white teammates in establishing himself, but to me it goes the opposite."

New York sportswriter Maury Allen said Erskine connected his experiences as a teammate and friend of Robinson with his son, Jimmy, who was born with Down syndrome.

"Jackie and Jimmy, because of tradition, superstition, ignorance, fear and arrogance felt the bitterness of rejection. Society considered them second class citizens or worse. The whole Robinson experience which I had lived through as a player, now seemed to arise in our lives. Jimmy was facing many of the same barriers. Only now I was coping with this experience as a father," Erskine wrote in his memoir, *What I Learned from Jackie Robinson.*

"Some of those who uttered these terrible words were people I personally knew quite well. I felt a good dose of the pain and rejection Jackie told me he used to feel. I'd never known how fearful people could be about someone who was different. I used to ask myself, 'why are all these harsh things being said about my son?' Jimmy didn't do anything to deserve this."

•　　•　　•

Erskine became a Dodger twice, initially signing for $3,500, only for commissioner Happy Chandler to rule that invalid because Erskine was still in the navy. It was a violation of baseball rules to sign an active serviceman. When Erskine left the navy in 1946, Dodgers executive Branch Rickey met with Erskine and his family to sign him again.

Erskine still needed a great deal of seasoning. The Dodgers asked him to pitch in Cuba that winter, but he told them he couldn't because he was getting married in November. Rickey convinced Carl to move the wedding up to October, and so began a great professional career.

Erskine was the other pitcher warming up in the bullpen in the Dodgers' 1951 playoff game with the Giants when manager Charlie Dressen lifted Don Newcombe and elected to bring in Ralph Branca. We'll never know whether Erskine would have prevented the greatest home run in baseball history, Bobby Thomson's Shot Heard 'Round the World.

Soon after, though, Carl emerged as the ace of the Boys of Summer, and he had crucial roles every time the Dodgers reached the World Series during his tenure. He started game two of the 1952 World Series, even though he almost couldn't answer the bell. Climbing off a stool after peering out the window of the trainer's room hours before the game, Erskine banged his knee into a heater, seriously aggravating a high school injury. He passed out from the pain and had to be revived. He still took the ball but suffered a 7–1 defeat.

In game five that year, on the day he was celebrating his fifth wedding anniversary, he allowed five runs to the Yankees in the fifth inning and out came Dressen. But instead of removing Erskine, the manager asked if he was taking his wife out to dinner that night to celebrate the anniversary. When a puzzled Erskine said yes, Dressen said to get the final out of the inning so the game would end before darkness fell. Erskine regained his command and pitched an eleven-inning complete-game victory, ending it with a strikeout of Yogi Berra as a finger blister tore.

Erskine started games one, three, and six in the 1953 World Series against the Yankees. He was shelled and lifted early in game one, but wheeled back for game three, in which he struck out fourteen to break Howard Ehmke's 1929 record. The Dodgers were down 2–0 going into game three.

"I wasn't shooting at any record out there—all I was aiming to do was get our backs away from the wall,"

Erskine told the *Brooklyn Eagle*. "To tell you the truth, I didn't have the foggiest idea that I had broken any Series record for strikeouts. I didn't know who held it and now that I found out that Howard Ehmke of the Athletics set the old record with thirteen strikeouts in the 1929 World Series, I'm still not sure that I can even spell that fellow's name right."

Erskine was a twenty-game winner in 1953, but it was the 1955 Dodgers that gave Carl his only Championship ring. However, in his only World Series appearance that October he allowed three runs in a three-inning no-decision. Nonetheless, he could appreciate the impact that title had, not only on a team but on a borough.

"It had so much significance," he told Peter Golenbock for his book on the Brooklyn Dodgers, titled *Bums*. "There was personal pride. There was a whole city that now could raise its head, look across the river to the Bronx and Manhattan and say, 'We're number one.' Everybody said, 'The ring.' Yeah, we got a ring, but it wasn't the ring. It was bigger than the ring."

Erskine summed up the sense of loss when the Dodgers left Brooklyn with a memory of one great fan, Captain Joe Dowd, a tugboat dispatcher: "He had lived through the eras of Brooklyn baseball probably back to the early 1900s. He knew a lot of history. He lived and died with the Dodgers. Gil Hodges and I got to be close friends with Captain Dowd and he'd take us and our families around the harbors in tugboats. It was beautiful. We'd go fishing with him in Sheepshead Bay and we got to be very close friends.

"Captain Dowd was nearly ready to retire and he geared his whole life around the retirement years when he could go to Ebbets Field every day, not just on his off day. The year he retired was the year we moved to Los Angeles, and it sort of typified the heartbreak of the Dodger fan for me to talk to Captain Dowd. He was broken-hearted and he never forgave the team for causing him to devote his life interest to them, and then without even asking him, they just left."

They went to Los Angeles. The first time Erskine entered the Coliseum, a reconfigured football stadium where the club would play until Dodger Stadium was constructed, he took one look at the left-field fence 249 feet from home plate and jokingly turned and started walking out of the park.

"Look at that monster," he said. "We should never have left New York."

Erskine was an All-Star in 1954 and he pitched no-hitters in 1952 against the Cubs and 1956 against the Giants. In the game against the Cubs, with an early threat of rain, manager Charlie Dressen came to the mound to tell Erskine to pitch quicker to avoid a rainout. Erskine walked the next batter, Willie Ramsdell, on four pitches. That turned out to be the only thing that kept Erskine from a perfect game. After a forty-minute rain delay, Erskine returned to the mound and retired every other hitter.

Erskine would later say the no-hitter against the Giants was the one that amazed him, because his arm hurt so badly he couldn't believe he was even able to pitch, never mind a masterpiece. He did have the added incentive of newspaper quotations from Giants scout Tom Sheehan saying that the Dodgers and Erskine were over the hill. After the game, Jackie Robinson taunted Sheehan with a copy of the article.

Don Drysdale, in his autobiography, *Once a Bum, Always a Dodger,* wrote that he looked up to Erskine as a veteran leader when he joined the staff.

"Carl Erskine was a prince," Drysdale wrote. "I never saw Erskine take a drink, never heard him utter one profanity. Erskine was the nicest guy in the world. . . . The only time I ever saw Carl get into any trouble was one day in L.A. when he was playing with a boomerang during batting practice. Walt Alston was by the cage watching Erskine in the outfield and Walt got angry. Batting practice came to a halt and Walt cussed out Erskine. Of all guys, Carl Erskine! That was the worst thing I ever saw Carl do. In fact, it might have been the worst thing Carl Erskine ever did."

Erskine retired during the 1959 season, the pain in his arm by then making pitching impossible. He finished 122–78 with fourteen shutouts and appeared in eleven games over five World Series. After he retired, Erskine became a businessman—when he wasn't coaching the Anderson College baseball team for twelve years. He sold insurance, ran a bank, and donated time to numerous state and civic institutions. Giving back became his trademark.

Time after time, Carl Erskine settled arguments between teammates, was a conduit between the clubhouse and the front office, and was a voice of reason for all. On baseball teams, players work, travel, and live together almost nine months out of the year. To have someone who was, as the apostles said, "fair and just, kind and merciful," meant that any player on the Dodgers had a man to could go to for peace and closure. To this day, Carl is as much a statesman for the game as he was a great pitcher.

THE PASSION
OF JACKIE ROBINSON

After my first experience as a bat boy, I always looked for Number 42. You can't really understand greatness at seven years of age, but there is an aura around someone like Jackie. Being seven that first day and twelve when my bat boy career ended, and living in the South, I understood that Jackie Robinson changed American society. He not only paved the way for African Americans to play baseball, he provided opportunity and hope for all minorities to pursue their dreams regardless of their race or background.

Jackie was a winner. He was relentless in everything he did, and his passion inspired those around him. Other players tried harder because he went all out, all the time. A meaningless spring-training game was no excuse for Jackie to give less than his best. He ran the bases with a vengeance. I sensed that Jackie had an almost psychic quality. He would sit in the dugout throughout each spring-training season and stare out at the mound. He would analyze every aspect of the pitcher's stance, his windup, and his delivery. He was a great student of the game. I would sit next to him and he would predict every single pitch. To a seven-year-old, this was like some circus act. But by the time I was twelve he had taught me to predict pitches. It was truly one of the greatest mental baseball skills I ever learned. To this day I do it as a parlor trick while watching a game, to the amazement of those around me. I have proudly passed it on to my teenage son, Ryan. He now has the gift. How we love Jackie Robinson in our house!

Robinson was the grandson of a slave and the son of a sharecropper. His father worked on a plantation for twelve dollars a month. Six months after Robinson was born, his father ran away with a neighbor's wife, deserting Jackie's mother and five children. They left the plantation for California, his mother working several jobs to make ends meet, his older sister running the house. In his autobiography, appropriately titled *I Never Had It Made,* Robinson admitted he was a member of a Pasadena street gang that confined its crimes to petty theft, nothing violent. But a neighbor and a neighborhood pastor encouraged Robinson to redirect his energies toward church work. By the time Robinson had become the first four-sport letterman at UCLA, he also was teaching Sunday school at church.

After a tumultuous stint in the military, including a court-martial proceeding in which he was exonerated, Robinson hooked on with the Kansas City Monarchs of the Negro Baseball League, although he called baseball "a pretty miserable way to make a buck."

Then came "The Noble Experiment."

Branch Rickey once told Robinson why he wanted to break baseball's color barrier. As a coach for Ohio Wesleyan in 1910, Rickey took the team to South Bend for a game, and the manager of the team hotel would not provide a room to a black player. Rickey negotiated for a cot to be placed in his room, which he would share with the black player, whom he found sitting on the cot in tears trying to tear the color off the skin of his hands.

Rickey never forgot what segregation did to the psyche of that player, or what it was doing to American sports and America in general. When he took over the Dodgers in 1943, he was determined to do something about it. He received the support of his club's board of directors and went searching for the ideal player to break the barrier.

Rickey sent his scouts on a worldwide search for that perfect player. Clyde Sukeforth, one of Rickey's top scouts and a former Dodgers manager, approached Robinson before a game at Comiskey Park in Chicago and asked if he wanted to play for a rival Negro League the Brooklyn Dodgers were planning to start. Robinson was skeptical, but he made a quick trip to Brooklyn to meet with Rickey. The club president then told Robinson he didn't want him for the new Negro League team, he wanted him for the Brooklyn major league team.

Rickey had thoroughly investigated Robinson's background, his character, his reputation. As the meeting progressed, Rickey explained to Robinson that what they were about to embark on was much greater than baseball. And the resistance they would face would be fierce. Rickey told Robinson he knew he would be a good enough ballplayer, what he didn't know was whether he had the "guts" to endure the hatred he would face, "no matter what happens."

"He knew I would have terrible problems and wanted me to know the extent of them before I agreed to the plan," Robinson wrote. "I was 26 years old and all my life back to the age of eight when a little neighbor girl called me a nigger—I had believed in payback, retaliation. The most luxurious possession, the richest treasure anybody has, is his personal dignity. I looked at Mr. Rickey guardedly, and in that second I was looking at him not as a partner in a great experiment, but as the enemy—a white man. I had a question and it was the age-old one about whether or not to sell your birthright.

"'Mr. Rickey,' I asked, 'Are you looking for a Negro who is afraid to fight back?'

"I will never forget the way he exploded.

"'Robinson,' he said, 'I'm looking for a ballplayer with guts enough not to fight back.' "

Robinson signed a Dodgers contract for a $3,500 bonus and a $600-a-month salary.

While at UCLA, Robinson met Rachel Isum, a nursing student who became his lifelong partner. What Gracie Allen was to George Burns, what Coretta Scott was to Martin Luther, Rachel was to Jackie, his rock, the love of his life. And it was a good thing because there was no way they could have made it through without each other. Jack and Rachel married a few weeks before Robinson's first spring training. Traveling from California to Florida, they encountered the kind of prejudice that would be their constant companion. Robinson received a chilly greeting from his new teammates, but the ice thawed with his first four-hit game for the Triple-A Montreal farm club. Fans in the stands, white and black, cheered Robinson's achievements. Robinson began to believe one of Rickey's predictions, that color didn't matter to fans if the black man was a winner. And Robinson immediately noticed that the composition of the crowd in the stands was changing, as an increasing number of black fans were attending to see the Dodgers' first black player.

But the prejudice and bigotry were everywhere. Clay Hopper, the Montreal manager, once asked Rickey if he really thought "a nigger's a human being." There were times when games were simply called off with no explanation. Or the explanations would be bogus, like the times when a day game was canceled because the stadium lights weren't working. Or when a game that had begun was interrupted when a policeman insisted he had to enforce a local law prohibiting interracial athletic competition.

Robinson won the International League batting title that year and the Royals finished in first place, advancing to the Triple-A World Series in Louisville, where that club's owners put a quota on the number of black fans who would be admitted. Robinson suffered through an o-for-11 slump and the Royals lost two of three games, but the club was warmly greeted when it returned to Montreal and proceeded to win three straight and the series, with Robinson's bat heating up to finish at .400. The Montreal fans carried Robinson around the field on their shoulders, a hero.

When Robinson reported to spring training the following year, he was told to move to first base. Although he had been primarily a middle infielder, Robinson was told by Rickey that the biggest need on the major league club was first base, and if he played well there in the spring, the media drumbeat would make his acceptance easier. Instead, returning Dodgers players began a revolt. As Robinson wrote in his biography, veterans Hugh Casey, Bobby Bragan, Dixie Walker, and Carl Furillo drew up a petition to keep Robinson out, but Rickey met with each instigator and ordered them to drop their opposition or leave. The petition drive collapsed.

Rickey gave Robinson marching orders for that spring training: to convince his future teammates he belonged in the major leagues by outplaying them in intrasquad games.

"I want you to be a whirling demon against the Dodgers," Robinson quoted Rickey. "I want you to concentrate, to hit that ball, to get on base by any means necessary. I want you to run wild, to steal the pants off them, to be the most conspicuous player on the field—but conspicuous only because of the kind of baseball you're playing."

Robinson hit .625 that spring, but Dodgers players still resisted. Rickey attempted to work the media through manager Leo Durocher, but that plan unraveled April 9 when Durocher was suspended by commissioner Happy Chandler for his "questionable associations" off the field. Rickey decided not to wait any longer. Figuring he could minimize the fallout from the Durocher decision with an announcement of even greater magnitude, just before an exhibition game that day he sent the press box a one-page release that read: "Brooklyn announces the purchase of the contract of Jack Roosevelt Robinson from Montreal. Signed, Branch Rickey."

Pretty much all hell broke loose and within a week Robinson made his major league debut, at first base, and his Hall of Fame career began with a deep offensive slump, followed shortly by a three-game series in Philadelphia during which Robinson received intense abuse from the Phillies' dugout at the direction of their southern manager, Ben Chapman. Robinson wrote that torment from trying to ignore the insults nearly sent him over the edge, but he remembered Rickey's admonitions and took it. He scored the only run in a Brooklyn win in the opener, which only escalated the abuse from the Phillies over the next two days until Robinson's teammate Eddie Stanky exploded: "Listen, you yellow-bellied cowards," Stanky yelled. "Why don't you yell at somebody who can answer back?"

This was the beginning of a special bond that developed between Robinson and his new teammates. The media quickly criticized Chapman and the Phillies for their intolerance. The commissioner's office warned the Phillies about racial baiting. Rickey later told Robinson that the Philadelphia incident was critical to the success of his noble experiment.

"Chapman did more than anybody to unite the Dodgers," Rickey said. "When he poured out that string of unconscionable abuse, he solidified and unified 30 men, not one of whom was willing to sit by and see someone kick around a man who had his hands tied behind his back—Chapman made Jackie a real member of the Dodgers."

But the ordeal had just begun. In May, *New York Herald Tribune* sports editor Stanley Woodward learned of a plot by the St. Louis Cardinals to strike if Robinson was allowed to play against them. Woodward exposed the plan and league president Ford Frick reacted swiftly, warning strikers that they would be suspended from the league and that Robinson's right to play was assured.

While there were still Brooklyn teammates who objected to Robinson's presence, there was also Pee Wee Reese, the shortstop and captain. Unlike so many others, Reese did not prejudge Robinson. He was a southerner, but Reese was a fair man, and he figured, if Robinson could help the club, that was fine with him. But Reese quickly became an active Robinson supporter and demonstrated it in Boston, when abuse coming from the Braves' dugout shifted from Robinson to Reese himself for being a white southerner playing with a black man. Reese called time-out during a game, walked over to Robinson, put his hand on his shoulder, and began talking to Robinson. The gesture of support silenced the hecklers.

As that season wore on, Robinson felt increasingly accepted.

"I started the season as a lonely man, often feeling like a black Don Quixote tilting at a lot of white windmills," he wrote. "I ended it feeling like a member of a solid team. The Dodgers were a championship team because all of us had learned something. I had learned how to exercise self-control—to answer insults, violence and injustice with silence—and I had learned how to earn the respect of my teammates. They had learned that it's not skin color but talent and ability that counts. Maybe even the bigots had learned that, too."

Robinson was an easy choice for Rookie of the Year, leading the league with twenty-five stolen bases and finishing second with 125 runs scored.

His second major league season came with different problems. He reported to spring training twenty-five pounds overweight after an off-season of banquet dinners held in honor of the National League's Rookie of the Year, an award that eventually would be named in his honor. He started that 1948 season in a horrible offensive slump, but heated up over the second half of the year to bat .296 and finish fourth in the NL with 108 runs scored.

He did all this despite the abuse and discrimination he was facing, on and off the field, while abiding by Rickey's dictum that he be man enough not to fight back. But by the end of the 1948 season, Rickey told Robinson, "You're on your own."

Here's how Robinson quoted Rickey in explaining the change of ground rules:

"I realized the point would come when my almost filial relationship with Jackie would break with ill feeling if I did not issue an emancipation proclamation for him. I could see how the tensions had built up in two years and that this young man had come through with courage far beyond what I asked, yet, I knew that burning inside him was the same pride and determination that burned inside those Negro slaves a century earlier. . . . So I told Robinson that he was on his own. Then I sat back happily, knowing that, with the restraints removed, Robinson was going to show the National League a thing or two."

That he did. Robinson said it was part revenge, but even more he just wanted to be himself. The notion of blacks in baseball had been established, as other teams began to sign Negro League stars and the Dodgers brought in Roy Campanella and Don Newcombe to join Robinson. Feeling liberated, Robinson had the best season of his major league career. He led the league with a .342 batting average and thirty-seven stolen bases, was second in both RBIs and runs scored, and was named the league's Most Valuable Player. The Dodgers that year fell just short in the World Series to the Yankees, losing in five games.

The next year was a particularly difficult one for Robinson, as his benefactor, Branch Rickey, was forced out of the Dodgers organization by new owner Walter O'Malley, who had been an officer in the corporation. Robinson claimed that O'Malley didn't like Rickey and, by association, didn't like Robinson.

"O'Malley's attitude toward me was viciously antagonistic," Robinson wrote. "I learned that he had a habit of calling me Mr. Rickey's prima donna and giving Mr. Rickey a hard time about what kind of season I would have."

Back in those days, club management had a very cozy relationship with the newspaper writers who covered the team. Not coincidentally, once Rickey left and friction developed between Robinson and O'Malley, Robinson's relationship with the New York media—particularly Dick Young of the *New York Daily News*—grew increasingly inflamed. Whether it was Jim Crow living arrangements at hotels or school desegregation in the South, Robinson had an opinion and wasn't afraid to express it. He believed his newfound outspoken nature didn't conform to O'Malley's perception of what a Negro ballplayer should be.

"I knew what O'Malley's problem was," wrote Robinson. "To put it bluntly, I was one of those 'uppity niggers' in O'Malley's book."

Young advised Robinson to be more like Campanella, who was happy just to be playing baseball and never considered himself a crusader for any other cause. Young told Robinson he was alienating the media because he was wearing his race on his sleeve.

"Personally Jackie, when I talk to Campy, I almost never think of him as a Negro," Young told Robinson. "Any time I talk to you, I'm acutely aware of the fact that you're a Negro."

Robinson didn't back down and explained he was proud of his color and of the accomplishments of black people in America and he wasn't going to change the way he acted or what he said.

Not even what he would say to O'Malley, who accused Robinson of faking an injury to miss a 1952 exhibition game, leading to a meeting between O'Malley, Robinson, and his wife, Rachel. O'Malley added fuel to the fire by also reprimanding Robinson for complaining about being assigned to a different hotel than the rest of the team. Rachel blasted O'Malley for not measuring up to Rickey.

"You know, Mr. O'Malley, bringing Jack into organized baseball was not the greatest thing Mr. Rickey did for him," she said. "In my opinion, it was this: Having brought Jack in, he stuck by him to the very end. He never listened to the ugly little rumors like those you have mentioned to us today."

Robinson got his digs in, too.

"It doesn't strike me as fair," he told O'Malley, "to have people who are sitting in comfort in an air-conditioned hotel lecture me about not complaining."

Robinson's tension with management, however, heightened when manager Charlie Dressen overplayed his contract negotiation and was replaced by Walter Alston in 1954. Robinson respected Dressen, but Robinson felt Alston "had a gut conviction that I resented his having taken Dressen's job."

As a bat boy, I was in no way privy to these high tensions. I only saw Walter O'Malley once when I was a kid. He was a stout man, with wire-rimmed glasses and a unique gruff voice. I could hear him before I could see him, but he had a presence that filled the clubhouse. Once I had signed with the Dodgers, Walter's legacy had grown and his significance among the other owners was well established. His vision for moving the team west and subsequent stadium and sponsorship deals made the Dodgers the premier franchise in baseball during the sixties, seventies, and eighties. I knew him to be fair, unbiased, and insightful. His son, Peter, graduated from the Wharton School of the University of Pennsylvania and spent time learning the business of baseball in Dodger minor league cities and, of course, in Dodgertown. He would take over the Dodgers as president in the 1970s and would excel as the steward for the family's franchise. Peter's conservative approach, his commitment to Los Angeles, and his desire to introduce baseball throughout the world, made him uniquely successful in the business and sports world. As an adult looking back and reading about Jackie's time with the Dodgers, I certainly understand a lot more about the circumstances surrounding Jackie than I did as a kid. Regardless, I'm compelled to convey my respect for the O'Malleys and all of the great things they did for Dodger baseball and baseball as a whole.

By the end of the 1954 season, Robinson began thinking about retirement. He was past his prime as a player at age thirty-five and had tired of battling the front office and the media. He put out feelers for a job in the private sector, but returned for the 1955 season, and that turned out to be a very good thing. Although his playing time was reduced during the regular season, the Dodgers reached the World Series for the fifth time since Robinson arrived, and this time they beat the Yankees in seven games. In game one of that series with the Dodgers trailing by two runs with two out in the eighth inning, Robinson took a gamble that would be unheard of today, stealing home.

As the 1956 season neared an end, Robinson found a future career path and negotiated a job as a vice president with Chock full o'Nuts, a coffee and food products company. He also gave *Look* magazine an exclusive on his retirement story, with the agreement that no story would be published until he could notify the Dodgers. When Robinson called general manager Buzzie Bavasi to tell him he was retiring, Bavasi first told Robinson he had been traded to the Giants for $30,000 and pitcher Dick Littlefield. Robinson couldn't tell Bavasi that he was retiring, that news would be delivered when *Look* published the story three days later. In 1962 he was voted by the Baseball Writers Association of America into baseball's Hall of Fame.

"Jackie made us better because of his ability and he made us closer because of his suffering," Snider wrote.

"The Dodgers helped to make him a Major Leaguer, and he helped to make us champions."

Robinson lived sixteen years after he retired from the game, dedicating his life to equal rights for all while battling diabetes, which took his eyesight. He held an active role in the marketing and promotion at Chock full o'Nuts. He was a tireless fund-raiser for the NAACP. He worked his way into politics, lending his credibility with an endorsement for Richard Nixon in the 1960 presidential race against John Kennedy, and later served in the presidential campaign of New York governor Nelson Rockefeller. When Rockefeller lost the nomination to Barry Goldwater, Robinson threw his support to Lyndon Johnson "because of the dangers of Goldwater politics." Robinson championed Johnson's support of the civil rights movement. "There is no doubt that President Johnson played a magnificent role in the political liberation of blacks," Robinson wrote.

He helped found the Freedom Bank, which would be operated by and for the black community. Robinson believed the advancement of blacks depended on "the ballot and the buck." And he endured the ordeal of having a child overcome drug addiction only to be killed in an auto accident at age twenty-four.

In 1997, Jackie Robinson's Number 42 was retired throughout baseball. No player would ever be given that number again, arguably the ultimate honor for an individual player of our national pastime. Jackie lived his life and played the game with passion. When you live with passion, it becomes the fiber of your character, and, in 42's case, the backbone of a society.

THE PERSISTENCE
OF DUKE SNIDER

Nicknames are often hung on people who capture our imagination, and the best nicknames need no further explanation. When someone says, "the Duke," he can only be talking about Edwin Donald "Duke" Snider. The Brooklyn center fielder was *the* power hitter of the Dodgers. If they needed a home run, the Duke was who they wanted at the plate. But he was more than a slugger. Defensively, Snider patrolled center field with an almost effortless grace. He carried that presence off the field as well. Mothers wanted their daughter to bring home the Duke for dinner. He was a matinee idol of a baseball player, long before there was an ESPN or an *Entertainment Tonight* to elevate an athlete to superstardom.

But Snider did not rely purely on his natural athletic ability. He was always looking for an edge, too. He told me that when he was at the plate, he would watch the outfielder shift and used that as an indication of where the pitcher would try to locate a pitch. He would say, "Watch the little stuff." And his "little stuff" would turn into big stuff. He still holds the Dodgers record for most World Series home runs (eleven). In my opinion, for a five-year period, he was the best center fielder in New York, and that wasn't easy when you had Willie Mays and Mickey Mantle finishing in a tie for second.

Basking in the Duke's presence each spring and watching his workouts and Hall of Fame hitting drills taught me the value of solid mechanics. Knowing that I was getting personal hitting tips from the Duke made me the envy of every kid in Drew Park Little League in Tampa.

Snider played eighteen major league seasons, the first eleven in Brooklyn, the next five in Los Angeles, then one year each with the New York Mets and the San Francisco Giants. He was an eight-time All-Star with six World Series appearances. He finished with 407 career home runs, had five consecutive seasons with at least 40 homers, six seasons with at least 100 RBIs, and six seasons with at least 100 runs scored, usually batting third in the order. He entered the Hall of Fame in 1980.

"His swing is perfect," Branch Rickey once said about

Snider, "and this young man doesn't run on mere legs. Under him are two steel springs."

Snider chose the Dodgers over the Reds and signed for a $750 bonus. His minor league apprenticeship was interrupted during World War II with a stint in the navy. When he reached Brooklyn, he wore Number 4, which he picked out because it was the number of his favorite player while growing up, Yankees first baseman Lou Gehrig. The most he ever earned in one season was $47,000.

Manager Burt Shotton made Snider the starting center fielder in 1949.

"When Shotton gave me that public vote of confidence by telling the press I was his center fielder, it did wonders for me," Snider wrote in his book, *The Duke of Flatbush*. "I became a consistent Major League hitter that year, with a batting average of .292, 23 home runs, 100 runs scored and 92 batted in."

But Snider was dogged by a tendency to strike out and another tendency to fret about it.

Striking out "kept gnawing at me," he wrote. "Maybe I was too competitive. I wanted to help the team win so badly that when I struck out, I felt it was not only a personal defeat, but that I had let my teammates down. I would be twice as determined on the next trip to the plate—and twice as uptight—and kept on digging myself into a deeper hole. So much of hitting is mental and self-control. The K's on the scorekeeper's scorecard continued to haunt me. It was like that for too many seasons in the early part of my career and years later my teammates still remember how I kept fighting myself."

Snider had a game in 1950 that he pointed to as a decisive moment in his career. He hit three home runs in the second game of a doubleheader and missed a fourth by two feet. He said the attention he received after that game from the media and the fans signaled that he was catching on with the public, and it helped bury his collapse against the Yankees in the previous World Series.

About that collapse. Snider had his breakthrough season as an everyday player in 1949, and the Dodgers won the pennant, advancing to the World Series and a date with the Yankees. First there would be a parade through Brooklyn, the hoopla and buzz of a city overwhelmed by an interborough rivalry, and Snider later acknowledged it got in his head. He started thinking too much and only magnified the pressure that already existed. The series would last five games, but Snider struck out three times with a pop-up in game one and was pretty useless the rest of the way.

"It was only the first game, but the nerves and insecurity of not knowing how I'd do in the next game sealed my fate for the rest of the series," Snider wrote. "It may have taken the Yankees five games to defeat the Dodgers, but it took them only one game to beat me."

Snider, the number three hitter in the lineup, hit .143 in the World Series, with eight strikeouts and no RBIs. He called himself "the goat" of the Series. But Snider said that even at his worst, he was able to come away from the series with a lesson learned. It happened in game three when he walked against Tommy Byrne and finally reached first base. He turned to Yankees first baseman Tommy Henrich and said: "Gee, I thought I was never going to get here."

And Henrich said, "Well, I wasn't going to pick you up and carry you down here."

Snider immediately understood the implication. He had to do it on his own. Coming from Henrich, the ribbing had even greater meaning, because of his reputation for delivering in the clutch. It was an attribute Snider aspired to.

"I knew after the '49 series I was going to have to be

more like Tommy Henrich to make my dream come true," he said. "Somehow, I had to become reliable too."

And he did. Snider described the 1952 World Series as "the Series of my deliverance." He joined Babe Ruth and Lou Gehrig as the only players to hit four home runs in one World Series. The Dodgers lost that Series to the Yankees in seven games, but Snider was no goat. He hit .345 with eight RBIs. In 1953, Snider had the first of five consecutive seasons with at least 40 home runs and he led the National League with 132 runs scored. In 1954, Snider contended for the batting title down to the final day, when Willie Mays emerged at .345, Don Mueller at .342, and Snider third at .341.

During the 1950s, the New York area boasted three of the best center fielders of that time, or of any time. Terry Cashman later wrote a popular song memorializing Willie, Mickey, and the Duke, his tribute to Mays, Mantle, and Snider. In his book, Snider said a fourth New York outfielder was probably the best of them all—Joe DiMaggio. But he wrote that the trio enjoyed the competition that the media created among them.

"We knew we were creating good box office for our teams and in every city where we played," he wrote. "All of us were successful, everybody was making money, so why should we mind?"

Snider always seemed to harbor doubts about his ability, so it was with great satisfaction that by 1955 he was being viewed by experts as the best of the best. Joe Sheehan of *The New York Times* wrote that Mays and Mantle "have a long way to go before they can put on the record that they measure up to Snider." Milton Gross of the *New York Post* wrote that there was "scarcely anything Snider cannot do better on the ball field than any other man in the game today." *Sports Illustrated* compared Snider to Joe DiMaggio.

The Dodgers were so good in 1955 that they had the top two finishers in the Most Valuable Player voting—Campanella finishing first and Snider second. Snider won *The Sporting News* National League Player of the Year award. And with Snider leading the league in runs scored and RBIs, the Dodgers went on to finally win their first World Championship, finally beating the Yankees in a seventh game after losing the first two games of the Series.

Snider hit .320 in the Series, becoming the first player in history to hit four home runs in two different World Series, and drove in seven. But it never came easily for the Dodgers against the Yankees, and this career high-light did not come without some hardship for Snider, who stepped on a sprinkler head in Yankee Stadium during game six and felt his knee pop, forcing him from the game six loss.

Snider wasn't going to miss game seven, and he recalls in his autobiography boarding the team bus at Ebbets Field for the drive to Yankee Stadium. Johnny Podres, the Dodgers' game seven starting pitcher, walked down the bus aisle telling his teammates, "Just get me one run today. That's all I'll need. Just one."

The Dodgers scored twice, both runs driven in by Gil Hodges.

Snider was one of the younger Boys of Summer and, although the Dodgers pushed the Yankees to another seventh game before losing the 1956 World Series, he sensed that the club had pretty much beat the buzzer on the time clock.

"Too many of the players who were the nucleus of our team for the previous 10 years were showing aging signs at the same time," he wrote. "Athletes, like every other group of people, vary greatly where the aging process is concerned. Some grow older sooner and faster than others. As an athlete, a certain time comes in your career when you stop being the type of player you were. You don't know when it's going to happen, but sooner or later you stop being the dominating force you used to be. When that happens you're on the other side of the mountain. That's where we were as a team. Jackie was thinking about retiring. Campy was looking at his 36th birthday. Furillo's legs were beginning to bother him. My knee was hurting more often. Erskine's pitching pains were worse."

On a barnstorming tour of Japan after the 1956 World Series, Snider heard reports of the Dodgers purchasing the Los Angeles Angels and their stadium in the Pacific Coast League. The California native assumed that meant the westward movement was about to include Major League Baseball.

Before the 1957 season started, Jackie Robinson retired. By the time it ended, the Dodgers had announced their move to Los Angeles. Robinson was thirty-eight, having squeezed out ten-year major league seasons after his years in the armed services and short stints in the Negro and minor leagues. Although Snider was a native Californian, leaving his adopted home, Brooklyn, was a bittersweet experience.

"Our roots there weren't as deep as they were in California," Snider wrote, "but they were just as strong."

Snider hit the last home run in Ebbets Field, and he asked manager Walt Alston if he could skip the last two games of the season, because he wanted that home run to be his last memory of the ballpark where he became a major leaguer. Snider didn't hide his sentiment.

"I was being torn away from my baseball home and I wanted to remember her that way," he wrote. "Walt understood."

A few years later, Ebbets Field met the wrecking ball. A longtime Brooklyn Dodgers photographer captured the sad event and sent photos to Snider, bringing him to tears.

"I saw the wall I used to aim at, the wall which Skoonj [Carl Furillo] and I stood in front of and leaped against, with the familiar signs of GEM razor blades and Esquire Boot Polish and the clock I cleared for my first World Series home run in 1952, the one that said, 'Bulova— official timepiece of the Brooklyn Dodgers,'" he recalled.

"Only the wall wasn't standing. In each picture, and in the ones of the grandstand and the bleachers, Ebbets Field was tumbling down under the impact of that big iron ball. I had worried about curveballs and fastballs and knuckleballs in that ballpark, but never had I ever worried with thoughts about a wrecker's ball. The good people of Brooklyn had lost their team. Now they had lost their last link to their Dodgers and to our past."

Because of his left-handed power stroke, no Dodger's game was affected more negatively by the move than Snider's. Walter O'Malley decided to move immediately, so while Dodger Stadium was being constructed, he arranged for the Dodgers to play at the Memorial Coliseum near the campus of USC. The Coliseum had hosted Olympic Games, as well as professional and college football, but, because of its oval configuration, never a baseball team.

The Dodgers had not set foot in the place before their 1958 season opener, having spent the entire spring-training exhibition schedule in Florida. Snider recalls being stopped by an excited Willie Mays as he made the walk from the clubhouse to the Coliseum field.

"Look where that right-field fence is, Duke," Mays said to him. "And look what they gave me—250 feet. They sure fixed you up good. You couldn't reach it with a cannon. You're done, man. They just took your bat away from you."

Snider then got his first look at the Coliseum layout and realized how right Mays was.

"I looked out at the view that was causing Mays so

much excitement and couldn't believe my eyes. My team-mates couldn't either. We saw a 'short porch' in left field, the closest outfield fence I'd ever seen, only 250 feet from home plate with a 35-foot green screen on top of it. Center field was 410 feet. Nothing unusual there. But right field was a story all its own. The fence was 402 feet down the line, compared to 296 feet in Ebbets Field."

Snider had knee surgery after the 1957 season, but the knee still bothered him in 1958, as did the dimensions of his new home field. He was able to play only 106 games, and his home runs dropped from forty to fifteen. But when he did play, he compensated by swapping power for average, climbing from .274 the previous year to .312.

It is Coliseum lore that Snider was once fined for trying to throw a baseball out of the place. It happened in June when he and teammate Don Zimmer struck up a conversation about how high the stadium rose. Zimmer asked Snider if he could throw a ball out of the stadium, and when Snider said he could, Zimmer rounded up bets from teammates, offering half to Snider if he succeeded. There were $400 in bets, and Snider's first attempt hit the top of the concrete railing, barely missing. The second throw fell a few rows short. On the third throw, the ball slipped and Snider's elbow popped.

It hurt so much he asked out of the lineup that game and general manager Buzzie Bavasi fined him $200.

Snider told Zimmer to hang on to the bets for a second round when his arm healed. Snider spent the last week of the season practicing long tossing and threw the ball out of the stadium on his first try. He won back the $200 and Bavasi also refunded the fine.

Snider wasn't the only player encountering a tough transition from Brooklyn to Los Angeles. The Dodgers finished in seventh place that year, and when 1959 started in the same fashion, Bavasi overhauled the roster. Among the additions were Maury Wills, Frank Howard, Ron Fairly, Wally Moon, and Tommy Davis. Erskine and Reese had retired and Furillo was playing part-time. Snider, Hodges, and Jim Gilliam were the only holdover starters from Brooklyn, and while the team lacked the superstars of the Boys of Summer, it played well enough together to win the Dodgers' second World Series in four years.

Snider called it in his book "one final curtain call for the boys from Brooklyn." Furillo, Hodges, and Snider all had starring roles in the Series win over the Chicago White Sox. Snider homered in the game six clincher, his eleventh World Series home run, triggering a six-run inning that sealed the deal.

Snider had been a Dodger his entire career, but as he aged and his skills declined, rumors that the Dodgers would trade him heated up. But Bavasi wasn't quite done with Snider. In 1962, he named Snider the team captain. The team had turned over to a younger group of players and Snider, who was the youngest of the Boys of Summer, was now the veteran imparting knowledge and leadership to the next generation while spending more time on the bench than in the field.

In spring training of 1963, Snider was sold to the Mets for $40,000, and Bavasi gave Snider $10,000 of that. Snider considered retirement, but Bavasi told him to go back to New York and get his four hundred home runs and two thousand hits, milestones to which Snider had long aspired. Snider returned to New York worried that fans would expect him to be the Snider of the 1950s.

Expectations weren't a problem for the Mets, who lost 111 games that year. Snider called it "a miserable experience." After sixteen years with one of the winningest organizations in baseball, Snider was with a loser. The following spring, after Snider asked the Mets to move him to a contending team, he was sold to the Giants, of all teams. He served mainly as a pinch hitter that year and retired at the end of the season.

Snider remained in the game after he stopped playing, first as a Dodgers hitting instructor, then as a minor
league manager. When Bavasi left the Dodgers to run
the Padres, he took Snider with him as a scout and
broadcaster, and Snider continued the latter role with the
Montreal Expos until his retirement.

In 1980, after an inexplicable ten-year wait, Snider
was voted into the Baseball Hall of Fame by the Baseball
Writers of America. Included in Ted Williams's remarks
were these:

"And the Duke. I wanna tell you, buddy—you are the
perfect example of what I've said about the writers for a
long time: They're not always right, because in your
case they were ten years late getting you here where
you rightfully belong."

When I think back on Duke's career and the struggles
he faced, and often overcame, with the move to Los
Angeles and the stint with the Mets, I'm reminded of a
moment early in spring training of 1983 with the Padres.
I had just joined them, and was jumping rope in the
secluded locker room about an hour before everyone was
scheduled to report. I was twenty minutes into the routine when I heard a voice say, "Hey, Garvey, what are you
doing?" The question came from a second-year player by

the name of Tony Gwynn. He was talented, but also always questioning and astute way beyond his years. "I'm buying time!" I said. "When you get over thirty, you will realize that you have to work harder to maintain what used to come naturally." Twenty years later, during Tony's Hall of Fame induction, he would give me credit for helping him realize the discipline you must have for success, and, in his case, greatness. I thank Duke Snider and the Boys of Summer for teaching me a lesson that I could pass on to a future Hall of Famer.

THE COMPASSION
OF ROY CAMPANELLA

I remember Roy Campanella as a three-time Most Valuable Player, the commander of the pitching staff, and a clubhouse leader. But I also remember him as the man who said, "Stevie, if you practice and study hard, someday you will be a Dodger."

Campanella was solid as a rock. He was more square than tall. He had incredibly strong hands and he perfected simple techniques for hitting and catching. His voice was soft, but deliberate when necessary. The tools of ignorance (as catcher's gear is known) were but a shield for this anchor of the Brooklyn infield. I have often used the very thing I learned from Campy throughout my life, and it's a life skill, not a baseball skill. When an argument would break out in the clubhouse, he would invariably say. "You guys can be wrong, but don't be loud wrong. Settle it now and get out on the field because we have a game to win." Campy brought the focus back to the "we" of the team and away from the individuals.

As great as Campy was as a ballplayer, Campy would show he was an even greater person through tragedy. A near-fatal car accident in Glen Grove, New York, left Campanella a paraplegic in 1958. What he did with the rest of his life took him from great to legendary in the minds of millions of fans and the general public. He would become a compassionate advocate for the joy of baseball. He entered the Hall of Fame at Cooperstown because of what he did on the field, but he lived the rest of his life like a Hall of Famer for humanity. Roy taught me to love the game for the game's sake and not to play for any selfish reasons. I learned about focus from Roy, who had to overcome racism at the start of his career and then physical challenges that most of us can't even fathom. Roy had the unique ability to play for the love of the game without any mental distractions. Those would have to wait for another time, because game time was for the team and for the fans.

I remember being in Wrigley Field in 1985, a full house of Cubs fans chanting, "Garvey Sucks," as I came to bat. They hadn't forgiven me from the previous playoffs, when I hit a home run that helped keep the Cubs from reaching the World Series again. Hey, it wasn't my fault. Lee Smith hit my bat. I didn't hear or feel a thing. Regardless, I had to play through the chanting. I only went four for fifteen in that three-game series, but the four hits included a triple and a home run. Campy gets some credit for that.

I was lucky enough to have known a healthy Roy Campanella. In the 1950s, he was the best catcher in baseball, perhaps in baseball history, which is what a lot of people who saw him play believed him to be. Maybe God had a higher calling for him, because Campanella became a source of inspiration to anyone paying attention.

In Ron Fimrite's moving 1990 *Sports Illustrated* profile about Campy, former teammate Joe Black talked about Campanella's amazing resilience.

"Now, there's a man who could truthfully say that life's kicked him squarely in the butt," Black told Fimrite. "He could be as bitter as anyone alive. But no. What you'll find instead is someone sitting there in his wheelchair smiling away and talking to everyone, reaching out to people and saying, 'Don't you dare feel sorry for me.' I had a friend of mine go up (to Campy) once, and he came back saying, 'Why, that man just makes you feel so important. He makes you feel good all over.' That's what he does, all right. He just touches your life."

Thinking about Campy in that wheelchair, it's worthwhile checking the stats to appreciate just how amazing a player he really was. By the time of his accident, Campanella had played ten years with the Dodgers, after a nine-year career in the Mexican and Negro leagues, starting at age sixteen. One can only guess the kind of numbers Campanella would have compiled if he had been allowed to play in the major leagues during those many years he spent in the other leagues, and if his career had not ended too soon.

As it was, he was a three-time MVP and an eight-time All-Star and played in five World Series. He could hit for average, finishing in the top ten three times, and for power, ranking in the top ten for home runs five different seasons. He led the league with 142 RBIs in 1953 and his forty home runs as a catcher stood as the record for forty-three years. When the new-age numbers crunchers computed his on-base and slugging percentages, Campanella finished in the top ten for on-base plus slugging percentage five times. If the Gold Glove had been around in his prime, he would have won a mantel full.

But on January 29, 1958, after working late at his

Harlem liquor store, Campanella headed out into a snow-
storm in a rental car because his regular station wagon,
the one with snow tires, was in the shop. The rental car
did not have snow tires, and about five miles from his
house, Campanella's car hit an ice patch, skidded into a
telephone pole, and flipped over. There were no seat
belts in 1958 and Campanella was tossed around, then
pinned under the dashboard. According to Fimrite's
research, emergency personnel responded to a call from
a local doctor and spent thirty minutes until they finally
righted the auto. There is speculation that the jolt might
have worsened Campanella's condition.

Doctors saved Campanella's life in an operation to sta-
bilize a broken neck and damaged spinal cord, but he
was paralyzed from the chest down. He spent three
months in the hospital, then six more months in a New
York rehabilitation center learning how to live confined
to a wheelchair until his death in 1993.

Campanella told Fimrite that he learned how to phys-
ically cope at the rehab center, but the psychological
adjustment seemed to come naturally to someone who
always saw the glass as half-full.

"Paralyzed people can get so depressed," he said.
"Thank goodness, that part of it didn't bother me. When

they put me in that wheelchair, I accepted it. For one thing, I was just happy to get out of bed."

Former teammate Carl Erskine related to Fimrite a visit with Campanella at the rehab clinic that further illustrated what Erskine called his "unbelievable spirit that just dumbfounds people."

"He started talking about his rehabilitation, how excited he was that they were going to give him the chance to lift a five-pound weight with his right hand," said Erskine. "And I remembered how strong that right arm once was, how many base runners I'd seen him throw out with it. There was a painting on the wall, a snow scene. When I looked at it, Roy told me with great enthusiasm that it was painted by one of the patients at the institute, a young boy who held the brush in his teeth. He was so proud of that boy. Roy just loves life, you see, and he's going to get out of it all there is."

Born in Philadelphia, Campanella had spent most of his life on the East Coast. But in 1957, at age thirty-six, after two down years with skeptics suggesting he was over the hill, Campanella was looking forward to moving West with the Dodgers to Los Angeles and the inviting dimensions of the Memorial Coliseum. Campanella told owner Walter O'Malley he intended to keep playing until the new ballpark opened. O'Malley had loaned Campanella the money to buy his liquor store and the catcher felt a strong sense of loyalty to his boss.

One of the great moments in Los Angeles baseball history occurred May 7, 1959, when the largest crowd in baseball history, 93,103, attended Roy Campanella Night at the Coliseum to honor their fallen catcher. The Dodgers convinced the Yankees to participate in this in-season exhibition game between the two clubs that had battled so fiercely in the World Series. In the middle of the fifth inning, Pee Wee Reese wheeled Campanella into the infield. As the other players surrounded them, fans were asked to light matches for Campanella and the stadium lights were dimmed.

Campanella lived in his wheelchair in New York for another twenty years until finally making the move to the West Coast, joining the Dodgers in a community-services role that included annual appearances at the Dodgertown spring-training complex, where he would gather the organization's catchers from the highest and lowest levels and hold miniclinics in an area dubbed "Campy's Corner."

One of his most faithful protégés was Mike Scioscia, who went on to catch for the Dodgers for thirteen years and then became a World Series–winning manager for the Angels.

"When he speaks, everyone listens," Scioscia told Fimrite. "He doesn't miss a thing. He'll come in the day after a game and ask me, 'Now why did you call for that pitch when the count was two and two?' What an amazing individual. He's gone through a life that none of us, hopefully, will have to endure, but he's come out of it so strong he makes all the rest of us look like wimps. I just thank God I've had the chance to know him."

Campanella told Fimrite he got as much from rejoining the Dodgers as they got from him.

"Down there, I put on my baseball shirt and my cap and I'm in this wheelchair and I'm going all over the place," Campanella said. "I get out early and work with the catchers, even the veterans. I don't care how old you are, you'll see something in this game you've never seen before. I tell them what I've seen. Oh, I ride around in my powered chair, all charged up, talking to everybody. I'm all charged up, that is, unless my batteries run down. This is my life, you know."

The same winter of Roy's accident, I lost my maternal grandfather, the man who moved the Garveys to Tampa. Having been to the funeral of a loved one, and then hearing from my dad that Roy Campanella could no longer walk, much less play, really opened my young eyes to the harsh realities of life. I went through a transition right along with the Dodgers in 1958. I realized that life was not simple, and that things, people, and places change. Change is the only constant in life, and we must adapt to it or get passed by.

Campanella was inducted into the Baseball Hall of Fame in 1969. Three years later, the Dodgers retired his uniform Number 39, along with Jackie Robinson's Number 42 and Sandy Koufax's Number 32. In 1974, Michael Landon made his directorial debut when he adapted Campanella's autobiography, *It's Good to Be Alive,* into a made-for-television movie. After Roy passed away it was hard to believe you were in Dodger Stadium without being able to look up and find Roy and Roxy, Campy's wife, sitting next to the press box on the club level. I still look for the wheelchair and expect to see him. It makes me feel better to think that Don Drysdale was just getting bored up in heaven, and now he has a catcher. In 2006, the Dodgers created the "Roy Campanella Award," voted by the club's players and coaches for the player who best exemplifies Campanella's spirit and leadership. Shortstop Rafael Furcal was the inaugural winner.

THE FAITH
OF SANDY KOUFAX

During each spring from 1956 to 1960 I would always see a tall, good-looking pitcher who seemed to have it all. I would watch him warm up and was amazed at the speed of his fastball and the break of his curve. The comments that I would hear were that he had this great talent but no real concept of how to pitch. Simply put, he did not have the control to be a big-time pitcher. What he did have was a quiet self-confidence that I would eventually understand to be faith. He had faith that was not only in himself, but in God.

Sandy Koufax spent six years in frustration, some games overpowering the opposition, others being the victim of too many walks and belt-high fastballs, and a lot of time just watching. Then in the spring 1961, his catcher, Norm Sherry, suggested that he take a little off his fastball and smooth his delivery. From that point on he became the most dominant pitcher in baseball. Sandy had perseverance, inner strength absolutely, faith unquestionably, and the stuff of greatness.

Let's talk in general about faith and in particular about Yom Kippur, the holiest day of the year in the Jewish religion. Sandy became an idol to any who believed in anything when he refused to pitch the first game of the 1965 World Series because it fell on Yom Kippur. I heard the classic line to describe the results—the Dodgers lost but Koufax won. To many around the world, Sandy's legacy is as much about what he refused to do as what he did on the mound. A man of few words led many by example.

In her remarkable biography—*Sandy Koufax, A Lefty's Legacy*—author Jane Leavy discussed at length the remarkable impact Koufax's decision had.

"By refusing to pitch, Koufax defined himself as a man of principle who placed faith above craft," she wrote. "He became inextricably linked with the American Jewish experience. As John Goodman put it in the movie *The Big Lebowski*: 'Three thousand years of beautiful tradition: from Moses to Sandy Koufax.' "

In her research, Leavy discovered that "the Jewish community laid claim to him, ascribing to him a religiosity he never acknowledged or displayed" and that he "remains a touchstone for measuring the progress of the Chosen People in the New World."

She spoke to rabbis and scholars and drew this conclusion: "The decision not to pitch was a transforming event, providing the catalyst for an unknown number of lawyers and Little Leaguers to acknowledge and honor their religion in like kind. Koufax made them brave. By refusing to pitch, he both reinforced Jewish pride and enhanced the sense of belonging—a feat as prodigious as any he accomplished on the field."

Of course, Koufax wouldn't have had that impact on society if he hadn't had such an impact on the game he played. Long before he found fame and fortune, he had a talent that was unmistakable. I remember Al Campanis describing what it was like the first time he saw a Koufax fastball, at a tryout at Ebbets Field in 1955.

"The first pitch he threw," recalled Campanis, holding his arms straight out, "made the hair on my arms stand up. The only other time that happened was the first time I looked up at the ceiling in the Sistine Chapel."

Koufax didn't like the endless travel required in his line of work, or the idle time between his starts or working nights. But that doesn't mean he didn't like his profession. He called those "irritations, the occupational hazards of a particular profession." The game itself, he said, he enjoyed. Pitching he loved. He loved it when it seemed effortless and he loved it when he had to battle to survive.

Koufax was born in Brooklyn to Jack and Evelyn Braun, who divorced when Koufax was three. He and his mother, an accountant, lived with her parents after the divorce. Six years later his mother met Irving Koufax. They married, and Irving Koufax became a strong father figure to Sandy.

In high school, it was basketball at which Sandy Koufax excelled, at least initially, not baseball. He could jump and had the body control to make moves in the air. If Koufax wasn't a dirty player, he at least was an aggressive one. He didn't mind hip-checking an opponent into the iron pole that held up the basket, although he believed it was possible that the arthritis that eventually ravaged his pitching elbow might have resulted from banging the elbow into one of those poles. Koufax earned a basketball scholarship to the University of Cincinnati, playing only his freshman season.

As Koufax wrote in his autobiography, as a pitcher he "came to the party late."

Ed Linn, the coauthor of that book, later put it like this in an article for *Sport* magazine while describing Koufax's role on the club in his early years: "If you thought of Koufax at all in those days—and there wasn't any reason to—it was only to confirm to yourself that the Dodgers were so strong that they were able to carry such a stiff."

In his first organized youth league, he actually was a left-handed catcher, taking a right-handed catcher's glove, turning it inside out, and relocating the strap. His second season, he was moved to first base. When he went out for the team at Lafayette High School, it was as a first baseman. The ace pitcher for the school was Fred Wilpon, who later became part owner of the New York Mets.

It was Milt Laurie, an opposing youth league manager, who saw the pitching potential in Koufax just by watching him throw the ball around the infield as a first baseman. He convinced Koufax to pitch for his team. Koufax had never pitched until he was fifteen and wasn't turned into a pitcher full-time until the age of seventeen. But it was Milt Laurie who changed the face of baseball history by turning Sandy Koufax into a pitcher.

Koufax enjoyed pitching, more than first base or

catching or even basketball. He enjoyed the fact that he always controlled the game, and even he could tell immediately that he had a gift, the ability to throw harder than anyone else. That became obvious when he threw a no-hitter in his second game.

Still, Koufax attended the University of Cincinnati on that basketball scholarship. While he knew that basketball would be the ticket to a college degree, what he didn't know was that the freshman basketball coach, Ed Jucker, was also the varsity baseball coach. When Koufax heard that Jucker was recruiting baseball players for a trip to New Orleans, Koufax volunteered to pitch. In his third start for the school, Koufax struck out eighteen and the scouts were drawn like a magnet. Ironically, one of the first clubs to give him a tryout was the Giants. Koufax went to the Polo Grounds and, as he put it, "hit the backstop more often than [the catcher's] glove." Fortunately for the Dodgers, he never heard from the Giants again.

Ultimately, Koufax was pursued by the Dodgers, Pirates, and Braves. His parents were puzzled about his intentions—academics or athletics?

"All I'm really sure of," Koufax told them, "is that if a major league club comes through with enough money so that I can go back to college if I don't make it as a pitcher—if I can get that kind of an offer and don't take it, I know I'll be kicking myself for the rest of my life for not giving myself a chance. I don't know how I know it, I just know it."

Koufax and his parents took a train to Pittsburgh for a tryout with Branch Rickey, who had previously run the Dodgers and was now at the helm of the Pirates. Rickey's son and assistant, Branch Jr., talked his father out of offering Koufax a contract.

While in Pittsburgh, Koufax had forgotten about a tryout that had been arranged with the Dodgers. It was rescheduled for September 14, 1954, at Ebbets Field. Rube Walker was the catcher and Koufax threw for nearly an hour. This was the tryout that reminded Campanis of the Sistine Chapel. But in case that comparison wasn't enough to make general manager Buzzie Bavasi authorize the bonus money, Walker was asked by Campanis for his assessment of Koufax and this was it: "Whatever he wants, give it to him. I wouldn't let him out of the clubhouse."

Koufax's father, a lawyer, made a handshake deal with Dodgers owner Walter O'Malley for a $20,000 bonus, to be finalized when the club cleared a roster spot. But

Koufax still had a tryout scheduled in Milwaukee, after which the Braves offered him $30,000. Koufax and his father, however, kept their word, and in December, after the club cleared roster room by trading Preacher Roe and Billy Cox to Baltimore, Koufax signed with the Dodgers.

At that time, any player signed to a bonus of more than $4,000 was required to be placed immediately on the twenty-five-man major league roster for two full seasons, regardless of his readiness to play in the major leagues. The intent was to discourage clubs from spending too much money on too many players with bargaining leverage. The unintended consequences, however, were to retard the progress of the most promising young players, because they basically became observers rather than honing their craft.

So it hurt those players, it hurt the club, and it definitely hurt the fringe player whose roster spot instead would go to the bonus baby. In Koufax's case, the player who was sent to the minor leagues was another left-handed pitcher.

"It took a Hall of Famer to keep me out of the major leagues," Tom Lasorda likes to say when explaining why he was sent back to Triple-A Montreal when Koufax was activated.

Koufax's first season was 1955, and in Dodgers history, it was the season of the Holy Grail. It was the Boys of Summer finally beating the Yankees for the organization's first World Series Championship. It was a dream season, but something less for Koufax. He wanted to pitch. Instead, he watched. He was the ninth pitcher on a nine-man staff, and his job was to pitch in blowout losses, and there almost weren't any for this team.

Koufax's debut wasn't until June 24 in Milwaukee, in part because of a sprained ankle that put him on the disabled list. A couple of wildly effective relief appearances earned Koufax a start, but eight walks resulted in a fifty-day gap before his next start. Manager Walt Alston was not fond of wild rookies with no minor league seasoning.

That next start came August 27, when sore arms had broken out all over the pitching staff. Koufax responded with a fourteen-strikeout, two-hit shutout of the Reds. It was the first victory of his professional career. He was nineteen years old.

The Dodgers would clinch the pennant that year earlier than any team in National League history and beat the Yankees in the World Series, while Koufax sat on the bench. Koufax had enrolled in a class at Columbia University, and after the seventh game he asked the professor if he could skip class to attend the victory party. The professor thought Koufax must be a huge fan, but Sandy explained that he was actually on the team. The professor had no idea.

The next year was even tougher for Koufax. Alston's lack of confidence in the bonus baby strained their relations, and the limited use hampered Koufax's progress.

"I'm not here to take pot shots at Walter Alston at this late date," Koufax told his biographer Jerry Mitchell for his 1966 book, *Sandy Koufax*. "Walt can stand on his record. I could even see his problem. Walt was hired in 1954, as everybody knew, to win not only a pennant but a World Series, the prize that had eluded Brooklyn from the beginning of time. In his first year he hadn't even won the pennant. The Giants had sneaked through and Alston's Dodgers finished third. In his second and perhaps crucial year, with the pressure on him to produce, they had saddled him with a bonus player. In his preseason planning he had to discount me. When his pitching, which had started so strong, began to crumble, he would have been less than human not to resent having me hung around his neck. He couldn't use me, Walt felt, and he couldn't get rid of me.

"I needed experience. I needed work. Walt needed to

win. I had always prided myself that I would come through in the clutch. Walt left me with the clear impression that he didn't think I had it in the clutch."

The Dodgers left Brooklyn for Los Angeles in 1958. They finished seventh their first year on the West Coast, but won it all in 1959, beating the Chicago White Sox. Opportunities for Koufax, however, were still few and far between, and when he did pitch, he was usually wild and ineffective. But there were those glimpses of utter brilliance, like the eighteen-strikeout masterpiece against the Giants in 1959. Koufax was a swingman that season, sometimes starting, sometimes relieving, still searching for that breakthrough.

"He had some of the same problems I had years before," teammate Duke Snider said. "He tried too hard and worried too much. He knew he was walking too many hitters, and those walks were eating at him the way strikeouts used to eat away at me."

At the end of the 1960 season, Koufax nearly made that breakthrough impossible. He thought about quitting. He cleaned out his locker after the season and gave equipment manager Nobe Kawano all of his gear. Kawano asked what Koufax wanted shipped to spring training.

"Nothing," he said. "Including myself."

"If you want to quit, go ahead," said Kawano. "But I wish you'd leave your arm."

"That summed me up pretty well," wrote Koufax. "Great arm; no head. All potential; no performance."

He had started that season 1–8 before a midseason turnaround helped him finish at 8–13. After that season, Koufax nearly made good on his thought of retiring before deciding to give it one last shot. In spring training in 1961, Koufax met with club statistician Alan Roth. Analyzing his 1960 season, Koufax concluded he needed to be more effective against left-handed hitters and throw more quality first pitches to each batter. On the way to a B game against the Minnesota Twins, catcher Norm Sherry urged Koufax to quit pressing, stop throwing, and start pitching. He pitched a seven-inning no-hitter.

"That day in Orlando was the beginning of a whole new era for me," Koufax wrote.

He opened that season 10–3, made the All-Star team for the first of six consecutive years, and finished the season 18–13 while breaking Christy Mathewson's fifty-eight-year-old record for strikeouts in a season with 269. He pitched the last home game played at the Coliseum, striking out fifteen in a thirteen-inning complete game that required a staggering 205 pitches.

The 1962 Dodgers shaped up as a powerhouse. Tommy Davis was a batting champ with 153 RBIs, Maury Wills smashed the stolen-base record with 104 and won the MVP Award, and Don Drysdale won the Cy Young Award with twenty-five wins.

Koufax started with an uncharacteristic four victories in April alone, but by May a numbness developed in the index finger of his pitching hand. The worse the finger got, the better he pitched. He even threw his first no-hitter, against the expansion New York Mets in the Polo Grounds, with that numb index finger. By the All-Star break, the numbness began spreading, and he had to abandon throwing the curveball because it had become too painful. He pitched eight games with the finger like that, compiling an 0.53 ERA, but by now it had turned the color of a red grape.

Medical testing concluded that Koufax had a blood clot in the palm of his hand, the result of getting jammed by a pitch while batting earlier in the season. After medication had cleared up the problem, team doctor Robert Kerlan told Koufax how lucky he was that gangrene had not set in.

The Dodgers club was not as lucky. After leading the league for nearly three months, they lost seven of their last eight in the regular season to finish in a tie with the Giants and lost a best-of-three playoff with San Francisco for the pennant.

Everything came together for the Dodgers and Koufax in 1963. The team swept the Yankees in the World Series. Koufax threw a no-hitter during the regular season and won the Cy Young Award. He pitched game one of the World Series, opposing Whitey Ford, and he beat the Yankees, 5–2, breaking Carl Erskine's single-game record with fifteen strikeouts. He also pitched a complete-game victory in game four, again opposing Whitey Ford.

In 1964, Koufax threw his third no-hitter, this one against the Philadelphia Phillies, which triggered a personal eleven-game win streak. But by the end of the season, Koufax's elbow had begun swelling and hurting. Dr. Kerlan diagnosed traumatic arthritis—more specifically, synovitis, or inflammation of the lining of the elbow joint. Fluid was drawn with a needle. Cortisone was injected and anti-inflammatory medication prescribed. It was a routine with which Koufax would become quite familiar. The condition was degenerative, meaning it would only get worse, not better, and would never heal. Koufax was shut down the rest of the season and the Dodgers finished tied for sixth place.

A winter of rest seemed to work wonders for Koufax's elbow, which showed no sign of the arthritis until the end of spring training, when it blew up again. Kerlan suggested that Koufax consider pitching only once a week. Koufax rejected that idea and just went back to pitching.

To say the least, it went pretty well. Koufax didn't miss a start in 1965. He won twenty-six games, pitched twenty-seven complete games, broke the single-season strikeout record, and pitched more innings than anybody in eleven years. Koufax insisted that, while pitching caused him pain afterward, his arm actually felt better during the games he pitched. Before games, Koufax would have his arm rubbed in Capsolin, a hot ointment that promoted circulation under the skin and provided a feeling of warmth on the skin. After pitching, Koufax would place his arm in a full-length sleeve made from the inner tube of a tire and submerge it entirely into a tub of ice water. When he was done drinking three beers, his treatment was finished.

For those who wonder how great Koufax could have been if his elbow hadn't gone bad, he had this dissenting view.

"If I have a weakness in my elbow, it is only reasonable to conclude that it is part of the same overall con-struction that gives me the ability to throw a ball hard," he wrote. "It all comes, after all, in the same package. I have unusually long arms, large hands and long fin-gers. The long arms give more leverage. The long fingers put an extra spin on the fastball and curve.

"The arm is a pretty good catapult. It is a catapult with a hinge, however, and pitching puts the hinge under enormous pressure. Since I have accepted all the advan-tages of this build without the slightest hesitation, I don't see how I can complain about the disadvantages."

There would be amazing occurrences in 1965 even before the World Series with the Minnesota Twins, like Giants pitcher Juan Marichal taking a bat to the head of Dodgers catcher John Roseboro, with Koufax arriving from the mound too late to prevent the attack. There was Koufax's fourth no-hitter, a perfect game against the Cubs that broke a tie with Bob Feller for most career no-hitters. There was the arrival of "Sweet" Lou Johnson, a journeyman who rescued the offense after Tommy Davis broke his ankle.

Then there was the World Series. The schedule called for game one to be played on Yom Kippur, the Jewish Day of Atonement. And Koufax would not be there, leaving that game to be pitched by teammate Don Drysdale. Instead, Koufax pitched game two, and here's what he wrote about it: "I had already pitched and lost the second game because of the coincidence of the opening game falling on Yom Kippur, a situation which I think was played all out of proportion. I had tried to deflect questions about my intentions through the last couple of weeks of the season by saying that I was praying for rain. There was never any decision to make, though, because there was never any possibility I would pitch.

"Yom Kippur is the holiest day of the Jewish religion. The club knows that I don't work that day. When Yom Kippur falls during the season, as it usually does, it has always been a simple matter of pitching a day earlier, with two days' rest, when my turn happened to be coming up.

"I had ducked a direct answer about the World Series because it seemed presumptuous to talk about it while we were still trying to get there. For all I knew, I could be home watching on television."

The Twins won the first two games in Minnesota. The Dodgers won the next three games in Los Angeles, Koufax winning game five. Minnesota beat Claude Osteen in game six. Manager Walt Alston didn't announce who would pitch game seven until the team arrived at the ballpark for the game. It was Drysdale's turn in the rotation. He gave the ball to Koufax, pitching on two days' rest, which Koufax would do eight times in his career. This was his third start in eight days. His arm was killing him and he had no curveball.

He threw his second shutout in four days and his twenty-ninth complete game of the season. And the Dodgers won the World Series.

The next spring, Koufax and Drysdale negotiated as a team and were represented by an agent, and when unable to reach an agreement with Dodgers management, held out of spring training, demanding a three-year deal and $1 million split between them. The holdout was originally planned by many more players and was fueled by Koufax's desire to be treated as an equal in salary negotiations. Koufax probably weakened his leverage by not acting solo. He probably generated an additional $2 million a year for the club, and he was willing to walk away from the game, which provided him the ultimate leverage.

Koufax was offered $100,000, Drysdale $85,000. They felt that the combination of what they did on the field (forty-nine wins in 1965) and their effect at the turnstile (attendance was well above average when they pitched) deserved better compensation. In the era of baseball's reserve clause, which bound players to a club for life, their tactics were revolutionary. On the eve of the season opening, Drysdale met with Bavasi and worked out an agreement all three parties could live with for the 1966 season. It was believed that the Dodgers agreed to pay Koufax $125,000 and Drysdale $110,000, but the players agreed to split the total, so they received $117,500 each.

All Koufax did that final season was win twenty-seven games and pitch twenty-seven complete games, winning the Cy Young Award and pitching the Dodgers into the World Series again. But he did it with an elbow that required cortisone injections every other start. Warned by doctors that he was in the process of becoming a cripple, he retired at age thirty-one and went to work for NBC as an analyst with a ten-year, $1 million contract. He walked away with five straight seasons leading the league in earned run average, four no-hitters, four World Championships, and a single-season record of 382 strikeouts.

He was no natural behind the microphone. And he found that he missed the game so much that he tried to come out of retirement in 1969 when Bavasi took charge of the new San Diego Padres, but the Dodgers obtained a ruling from the commissioner's office making Koufax ineligible for the expansion draft.

I have seen Sandy over the years, always well dressed, always affable, and seemingly etched in time with handsome looks and a charming smile. That in itself doesn't make the man, but a quiet faith in who you are, what you've accomplished, and how you can affect others does.

THE FORTITUDE
OF MICKEY MANTLE

There weren't enough hours in a day for my mom, Millie Garvey, to lecture me on how to behave in the presence of Yankee greatness. To Millie, even the grounds crew possessed greatness for the mere fact that they had a job with the Yankees. Millie Garvey loves her boys in pinstripes! It wasn't a total loss in Mom's eyes when I played against the Yankees and lost two out of three championships. Mom simply said, "May the best team win." That's loyalty. The Yankees were baseball royalty and still are in her eyes. What a thrill when not only her husband drove the Yankee team bus but her son actually interacted, shook hands, handed them their magic bats, and held their rosin bags. It doesn't get any better if the pope lets you kiss his ring, she would say. That first time I went as a bat boy for the Yanks was the longest day of Millie Garvey's life, waiting for us to come home. I needed to use my eyes as cameras, taking yet another picture with every blink. Yogi was warm and welcoming, willing to put up with a kid. My mom made sure I called him Mr. Berra. I now can say I have known him for fifty years. Even if I was just another kid to him, he was tremendous in my life. These days, when I am in Yogi Berra's presence, like all the other greats, I pretend I belong, like I'm one of them, but to tell the truth I still feel like that bat boy honored and humbled to be in the presence of such greatness. I always think back to the days of seeing them for the very first time and how that felt. Now let me tell you about Mr. Mantle.

If those previously mentioned are the Boys of Summer, as author Roger Kahn dubbed the Dodgers of the 1950s, "the Mick" is where you separate the boys from the men. The late Billy Martin said, "No man in the history of baseball had as much power as Mickey Mantle. No man. When you're talking about Mickey Mantle, it's an altogether different level."

Ironically, Mickey would hate being singled out and separated from other players. With his "ah, shucks" southern humility, this consummate teammate would most want to be remembered for his ability to bring a team together. What this bat boy remembers is walking

into the locker room at Al Lopez Field in Tampa and seeing a specimen of a man. At age nine I knew of his greatness, but to see him in person, can you imagine? There
he was; I was sharing the same air. Forget about the fact
that I was getting to be his bat boy. Are you kidding me?
I hadn't felt that way since my first puppy. I peed when he
patted me on the head.

He had this thick neck, huge biceps, a strong chest,
and powerful thighs. Mickey was wrapping Ace band-
ages around both knees. He got up slowly, wincing as he
stretched his torso and put on the famous Number 7. He
would later take batting practice and hit prodigious
home runs over the light towers. Successful major
league players would stop and watch in awe as Mickey
slugged pitch after pitch, farther and farther. I love, to
this day, mimicking his swing and showing my boys
how the great one did it—in theory, that is. I loved his
home-run race in 1961 with teammate Roger Maris and
how he stood up for his teammate when fans and the
press took shots at Maris because he was about to break
the single-season record of sixty home runs set by the
legendary Babe Ruth. What a class act Mickey Mantle
was, truly a man among boys.

Though he was gifted with exceptional strength and

athletic ability, Mantle's life was also haunted by physical limitations. When he approached historic and mythical proportions as a high school athlete in Oklahoma, he suddenly developed osteomyelitis, bone inflammation, triggered by an infection. Even though he would overcome this difficult disease, accidents and alcohol humanized his achievements and endeared him to millions of people.

So, what was the greatest lesson learned from what I believe was the greatest hitter of all? To play through the pain, of course. I don't think I would have set the National League consecutive-games-played streak without the Mick's lesson of pushing through the pain. Thanks, Mickey. If one's greatest success is measured by the ability to overcome adversity, the Mick finished second to none.

Mantle was born during the Depression in Oklahoma. His father worked in the zinc mines during the week and played semipro baseball on the weekends. Mantle believed his father had major league talent, but he never got that chance. His son did. The elder Mantle named his son after Mickey Cochrane, the Hall of Fame catcher. When Mickey was old enough to hold a bat, his dad would pitch tennis balls right-handed and have his son bat left-handed; Grandpa Mantle would pitch left-handed and Mickey would hit right-handed. That's how he learned to be a switch-hitter, even though he initially was uncomfortable batting left-handed. His father understood that managers tended to platoon players who couldn't hit both righties and lefties. What little extra money his father earned often was spent on new gloves. They practiced every day.

The first injury Mantle could remember suffering came about in a high school football game when he was kicked in the shin. When the swelling didn't go down, a specialist diagnosed osteomyelitis and recommended amputating the leg, but Mantle's mother wouldn't allow it. The new wonder drug, penicillin, cleared up the infection, and after a few months Mantle was able to resume sports.

While playing semipro ball at age seventeen, still in high school, Mantle was noticed almost by accident by Yankees scout Tom Greenwade while he was scouting one of Mantle's teammates. Greenwade told Mantle he'd return when he graduated from high school and not to sign with anyone else. On graduation day, Greenwade returned and signed Mantle as a shortstop to a $1,100 bonus. Mantle took the money and bought a used car. Greenwade would say Mantle was the best player he ever saw, but probably not the best shortstop. Mantle started professionally at Class D Independence, where he hit .313 his first season but also committed forty-seven errors. That winter, Mantle was summoned by the draft board, but the X-rays revealed osteomyelitis in his leg and earned him a 4-F exemption from service.

He graduated to the Class C Joplin Miners in 1950, managed for the second season by Harry Craft, who saw Mantle's prodigious power and urged management to move the kid to the outfield. That second professional season, Mantle hit .383, and on the bus ride home after the last trip of the season, Craft told Mantle he would be called up to the New York Yankees for the final two weeks of the season. As a shortstop. A scared, eighteen-year-old shortstop.

When the season and his brief call-up ended, Mantle returned home and went back to the mines. He showed up late for his first spring training because his ticket never arrived. The club claimed it didn't know how to reach him. When he arrived in Phoenix, he caught the eye of manager Casey Stengel, not with his legendary power but with a tool equally excellent—his speed. He lined up for the traditional rookie hundred-yard dash and won by ten yards.

"Look at that kid run," said Stengel. "Let's find out some more about him."

The more Stengel learned, the more he liked. Likewise, Mantle accorded Stengel the respect due a father figure.

Mantle's running speed led to an immediate shift to the outfield, and his torrid bat in exhibition games earned him the kind of expectations that would have spelled doom for a lesser talent, as he realized after an exhibition game against the University of Southern California in Los Angeles.

"I lived up to the press notices by hitting two homers, a triple and single," he wrote in his 1985 autobiography, *The Mick*. "Half the student body must've been in the stands and it seemed as if every one of them came heading toward me as I walked out of the locker room. Absolute bedlam. They shoved scraps of paper into my hand for autographs, clawed at my shirt, pushed and screamed. It shook me. Yea, I finally realized the price I might have to pay for being called the next DiMaggio."

Mantle hit .402 that spring and the Yankees had no choice but to keep him on the roster, even at age nineteen, jumping straight from Class C ball. On Opening Day at Yankee Stadium, Mantle was in the three hole, between

Phil Rizzuto and DiMaggio, in front of a crowd of fifty thousand, twenty times the population of his hometown of Commerce. It was the start of a Hall of Fame career.

For Mantle, there was plenty of doubt and a little homesickness. "It didn't come as easy as they wrote," he remembered. "The New York fans were led to believe some kind of Superman had arrived on the scene. He was going to hit ball after ball over the center field bleachers, clear into the Harlem River. He was another Ruth, another DiMaggio, maybe better than both. But I was neither. I had enough trouble trying to be Mickey Mantle."

Mantle went the first month of his major league career without a home run. He started to press and that made things worse. By midseason, Mantle had been sent down to the minors. The slump continued until Mantle's father, hearing the despair in his son's voice over the phone, came to town and challenged his son to bear down. The following series Mantle started a stretch of eleven homers in forty games, and he was back with the Yankees by the end of August.

By the time Mantle made the major leagues, his father was ailing from years spent in the zinc mines of Oklahoma. The 1951 World Series should have been memorable for Mantle because it was his first, but it turned into something unfortunately unforgettable. Chasing a pop fly between him and DiMaggio, Mantle committed to the ball, knowing that DiMaggio was favoring a sore heel, but at the last minute he was called off by DiMaggio and slammed on the brakes, his spikes catching on the rubber cover of a drain hole in the grass. Mantle's right knee popped. While his teammates were winning the World Series, Mantle underwent surgery to repair torn ligaments. While Mantle was in the hospital, so was his father, who was diagnosed with Hodgkin's disease. His father died the following year at age thirty-nine.

By May of the next season, Stengel made Mantle the starting center fielder. And Mantle was a gamer. Mantle had his breakthrough season in 1952, his first season as an everyday player. He batted .311, was an All-Star for the first of fourteen consecutive seasons, finished third in MVP voting, and made it through a World Series–clinching celebration without injury.

But Mickey being Mickey, when he got home to Oklahoma he wanted to have some fun. So he set up a basketball team that played exhibition games. On a fast break he twisted his knee and needed surgery to remove a piece of cartilage. He arrived at spring training with a limp and one thing led to another.

"I began favoring the leg," he wrote, "which eventually weakened the other knee and led to pulls and strains elsewhere. The arms, the shoulders, the back—they dogged me season after season."

After the 1953 season, Mantle had another knee operation, this one to remove a cyst. But he seemed good as new in 1954, when he hit .300 and drove in more than a hundred runs for the first of four times. The Yankees reached the World Series again in 1955, but lost to the Dodgers in seven games.

It wasn't until 1956 that Mantle truly fulfilled the expectations of greatness. He became only the fourth player to ever win a Triple Crown—leading his league in average, home runs, and RBIs—joining Hall of Famers Rogers Hornsby, Lou Gehrig, and Ted Williams. He won the first of three Most Valuable Player Awards. He said the highlight of that season was beating out Williams— "my number-one idol, the greatest hitter I ever saw"—for the batting title. In the World Series, the Yankees paid back the Dodgers for the previous year, with Don Larsen winning one of the games with the only perfect game in World Series history. Mantle helped win that game with a home run and an over-the-shoulder catch of a Gil

Hodges drive that Mantle said was one of the best plays he ever made.

In addition to the fifteen All-Star seasons and three MVPs, Mantle won the Silver Slugger, a Gold Glove, one batting title, and one RBI title. He led the league in runs scored six times, total bases three times, and home runs four times. His Yankees won seven World Series. And when asked what he'd want on his tombstone, he said, "A great teammate," which is what was engraved there.

But he couldn't stay healthy. In the seven-game World Series loss to the Braves in 1957, Mantle suffered an injured right shoulder when Red Schoendienst landed on him during a pickoff attempt. The injury required another off-season operation. But the Yankees exacted revenge against the Braves in the World Series the following year.

The Yankees went the other way in 1959 and Mantle struggled as well. That off-season, the Yankees traded for Roger Maris, and the two would put on an amazing home-run derby in 1961.

But first came 1960. For Mantle, it started with his annual salary dispute with general manager George

Weiss that ended with a humiliating pay cut. Mantle overcame the depression caused by the flap and finished the season with forty home runs, one more than Maris, who led the league in RBIs and was named MVP. The season ended, of course, with Bill Mazeroski's walkoff home run that gave the Pirates the World Series win over the Yankees.

"Nothing ever hurt as bad as that one," Mantle said. "In all my World Series experience, that was the one time when I really thought the better team had lost."

The 1961 season was one of the most amazing in the history of baseball, and Mantle had a front-row seat to the home-run derby.

"The single greatest feat I ever saw was Roger Maris hitting his 61 home runs to break Babe Ruth's record," Mantle wrote. "I was with him practically every step of the way and I know the dues he paid to get there."

Mantle had made a run at Ruth's mark in 1956 and endured the media circus it triggered. But as Mantle explained, he had been under scrutiny from the day he originally signed. Maris was a different story. He was private and uncomfortable with the attention.

Maris broke Ruth's record with sixty-one homers. Mantle finished with fifty-four, but it could have been a lot closer. With eighteen games to play, Mantle trailed by three and came down with a bad cold. Broadcaster Mel Allen advised Mantle to see his doctor, who gave Mantle a shot, which led to an infection, and Mantle missed most of the last two weeks of the season.

Mantle won the MVP Award in 1962 despite missing a month with another serious injury, pulling a hamstring in his left leg trying to leg out an infield hit, then blowing out ligaments and cartilage in his right leg when he kept trying to run. He missed a month. His 1963 season was ruined when he suffered a broken left foot running into the fence chasing a Brooks Robinson fly ball. Mantle missed sixty-one games. That was the year the Yankees were swept by the Dodgers in the World Series.

Yogi Berra took over as manager for Ralph Houk in 1964. The Yankees fell one win short of winning the World Series against the Cardinals. Then Berra was fired, replaced by Johnny Keane, and the Yankees finished sixth in 1965.

By this time, the injuries were really taking a toll on Mantle's body, and now Bobby Murcer had arrived with the billing of "the next Mickey Mantle." Things didn't get better when Mantle reinjured his right shoulder while playing touch football with his brothers and sons after the 1965 season. Surgery was performed at the Mayo Clinic to remove bone chips and calcium deposits.

The waning years of the sixties saw Mantle and the Yankees go in the same direction. Both tailed off. Mantle had a lesser supporting cast and couldn't do it himself. In 1967, Mantle moved to first base to take some of the stress off his legs. His final season was 1968. He hit .237. Having decided it was time to retire, Mantle showed up in Florida before the Yankees reported for spring training and, just to be sure, tried to work out. He couldn't do it. On March 1, he announced his retirement at age thirty-seven. In 1974, Mantle was inducted into the Hall of Fame alongside teammate Whitey Ford, calling it "the biggest moment of my life." In Mantle's autobiography, he wrote that he still was a baseball fan and enjoyed watching players like Tommy John, George Brett, Pete Rose, and he even mentioned me.

THE PERFECTION
OF AL KALINE

Having served as a bat boy for the high-profile Dodgers and Yankees, I was not really awed in the presence of the Detroit Tigers in the spring of 1958. They had a storied history as well, with some great players, but no real superstars at that time. My dad's assignment transferred to the Tigers, and going to the bus just wasn't as exciting that year. My father, however, mentioned to me that Number 6, Al Kaline, had won the Rookie of the Year Award the previous year, and he played the game as it should be played, so I should watch and learn.

I would later realize that Kaline had an uncommon skill and grace that simplified the complicated game of baseball. That first day, Al made me a fan for life. In four at-bats, he singled to right, homered to left, pulled off a perfect hit and run, and drew a walk in an at-bat that lasted twelve pitches. In the field, he glided to the balls hit to the left or right. I remember when one was hit over his head, he gracefully went up with two hands and caught it, pivoted, and fired a bullet to second base. Al's play was a thing of beauty. He just made everything look so easy. Everything was done to perfection, as if Al had written the book on the mechanics of baseball.

Like Mickey Mantle, Al Kaline also suffered from the rare disease osteomyelitis. An operation took two inches of bone from his leg and doctors speculated about whether he would be able to walk normally, much less run. But with a single-minded determination, he would walk and he would run, to perfection.

By watching him over the years I learned that we can never be satisfied with our accomplishments. He made me a player who wanted to do endless drills and stay in optimum shape. The endless pursuit of the perfect game, the sweet spot in time when all hard work comes together in execution, pushed me to find out how good I could get. I was honored to also wear the Number 6, sharing it with one of my heroes. Even though I idolized Lou Gehrig and his consecutive-game streak, Al Kaline was the one ballplayer that I could relate to in terms of preparation and execution on a daily basis. I remembered Al frequently during my own streak of 1,207 consecutive games, which became the National League record. You have to truly love the game to want to play every day, every inning, through pain and failure. Like Al, I had a passion for doing everything I could and striving for perfection.

Al Campanis, the Dodgers general manager, liked to say that "the good ones come fast," and he was talking about players like Kaline. The son of a Baltimore broommaker and semiprofessional catcher, Kaline originally was trained to be a pitcher but preferred to hit. What he lacked in physical frame he made up for in determination. He played football in high school until he fractured a cheekbone, and he also made the basketball team, but he would excel at baseball. He had a powerful and accurate throwing arm from center field and a naturally smooth batting stroke.

After his freshman season, Kaline had a tryout with the Brooklyn Dodgers, but a scout told him to come back when he gained some weight. He listened to the advice and added 20 pounds of muscle for his sophomore season, all the way up to 135 pounds. By then, the Dodgers weren't the only team aware of Kaline. He landed on the radar of a Tigers scout and by the time he was a junior he was up to 160 pounds. The day after he graduated high school, he signed with the Tigers for a $30,000 bonus, which he gave to his parents so they could pay off their house and cover costs of eye surgery for his mother.

As a bonus signing, Kaline was required to remain in the major leagues for two years or the Tigers would risk losing him to another team in the draft. His second day as a major leaguer, manager Fred Hutchinson came over to Kaline in the eighth inning and told him he was going in to play right field, a position he had never before played. Hutchinson used Kaline judiciously that first year, more interested in getting the nineteen-year-old acclimated to the big leagues.

Hutchinson introduced him to Ted Williams, who watched Kaline bat, lectured him on how to improve his game, and gave this answer when Hutchinson asked if he reminded Williams of anyone, as chronicled by Al Hirschberg in *The Al Kaline Story*.

"DiMaggio," Williams said. "He's got the same stance, with his legs wide apart and the same swing and the same confidence. 'Course, Joe was in a class by himself, but this boy could be as good."

Kaline spent his first off-season following Williams's advice on exercise—swing a weighted bat and squeeze a hard rubber ball—to strengthen his hands and wrists, and coming out of his first spring training, Kaline won the starting right-field position for the Tigers. The day he threw out three runners on the bases from right field, Kaline became a hometown star.

"You've got to see this boy every day to appreciate him," said coach Jack Tighe. "He has absolutely perfect coordination. He warms up like a pitcher before every inning and when he throws, every muscle ripples."

By Kaline's second season, he had the most respected outfield throwing arm in the league. After Kaline stole a potential home run from Mickey Mantle, DiMaggio said this: "This kid can't miss being one of the greatest all-round ballplayers of all time. He's got that extra special look that you hear about but seldom see."

In his second full season, 1955, Kaline hit .340 to become the youngest batting champ in American League history, a title previously held by Ty Cobb. He was runner-up for MVP while playing for a fifth-place team. He spent the winter working in a sporting-goods store, and the next season the Tigers more than doubled his salary, to $26,000.

Kaline once said his remarkable second season was "a

handicap" because it created unrealistic expectations, and he slumped in his third season for the first time in his career.

"I realized that I knew very little about the science of hitting and almost nothing about the men who were being paid to get me out," he wrote. "For me, that was the real beginning of my education as a baseball player."

He began studying opposing pitchers and seeking advice from older teammates.

"For the first time, I had a pretty good idea what I was going to see even before I stepped into the batter's box. Then, and only then, did I begin to develop the real confidence in myself and my ability to walk up to the plate and outthink a man who was getting darn good money to outthink me. Once you start thinking about your hitting, then you know you're beginning to grow up as a ballplayer."

At age twenty-four, Kaline received praise from a new management team.

"Kaline is far and away the best defensive right fielder I've ever seen," said manager Bill Norman. "Nobody else is even close to him. And as a hitter, he's the answer to a manager's prayer."

"He's only twenty-four, but he's got the poise and

savvy of a man ten years older," said general manager Rick Farrell. "He's matured just since last year and now he's a better ballplayer than ever."

When Harvey Kuenn was injured, Kaline became the emergency center fielder and immediately drew comparisons to Mickey Mantle and Willie Mays. When Kuenn returned, he went to right field and Kaline stayed in center.

"I was lucky. I got the chance to play regularly early," he wrote. "But I've often wondered what it would have been like if I hadn't."

In 1960, Kaline went through the worst slump of his career, which led to what he considered the greatest lesson of his career.

"I learned the importance of confidence to a professional athlete, a lesson I will never forget," Kaline told *Sport* magazine. "A big-league ballplayer, who knows he can hit and has hit well before, must never let himself lose faith in his ability to hit well again—regardless of how long any slump may last. For me and every other major leaguer who takes his baseball life and work seriously, confidence is a secret strength.

"Without it, many ballplayers who could develop into outstanding hitters and pitchers never realize their true potential. Confidence is an intangible, something that's almost impossible to see, but it can make or break a hitter or pitcher and it can make or break a team."

After two off years and another change in management, Kaline was moved back to right field in 1961. New manager Bob Scheffing called on Kaline to assume a leadership role in the clubhouse as well as the lineup.

Skeptics wondered if Kaline was over the hill, but he worked harder than ever in the off-season and came to training camp revitalized and committed to proving them wrong. Hooked up in a seesaw battle until September, the Tigers faded and the Yankees won the pennant again, but Kaline was vindicated with a .324 average. He also noticed that he struck out only forty-two times that year, which he took to mean that he wasn't swinging aggressively enough. Despite missing two months of the next season with a broken collarbone, Kaline set a personal best with twenty-nine home runs, ten more than the previous year.

In 1963, Charlie Dressen, the former Brooklyn Dodgers manager, became the eighth skipper for whom Kaline had played.

"This Kaline is better tired than most guys are fresh," Dressen said. "He's absolutely the best right fielder I've ever handled, and maybe the best ballplayer. I always thought Jackie Robinson was the best who ever played for me. Jackie played hard and could do so many things to win a ball game for you. Kaline is the same way."

Kaline played twenty-two years, finished with 3,007 hits, 399 home runs, and a career batting average of .297. He had a great throwing arm, strong and accurate, and he was clutch enough to hit .379 in the 1968 World Series.

I have seen Al several times over the last forty years. Each time he has been gracious and cordial, always taking time to talk and share that special interest that comes with having played the sport. There is a bond between generations and eras, characters and personalities, among those blessed with the talent to have played baseball at the major league level. But what separates the good ones from the great ones is that quest for perfection. Al seemed to understand that if you do not reach for the ultimate goal, whether on the field or off, you will never find out just how good you can be.

THE LAST DAY

My last day as a bat boy was at Tampa Stadium, Dodgers versus Reds. I was playing on a Pony league team and practicing several days a week, so my opportunities to join Dad for an off day from school and practice were rare. But I remember roaming around in the clubhouse after the game, picking up wet towels and bags full of crusts from eaten sandwiches as Koufax, Drysdale, Wills, and others walked by. I looked out the main door and saw my dad greeting each player and taking their bags just like the first time five years earlier. I realized that here I was, an insider of sorts, actually part of this team in a small way. Five years older, I understood a lot more than I did when I started my bat boy journey. My dad was on the outside, waving to me with a smile only a dad can give that says, I wouldn't have it any other way. How lucky I was! Just a kid who got a chance to be close to greatness. To learn from the best, not just how to play the game, but how to live life with grace and character. Even their flaws, which made me blush as a kid, didn't change the greatness of who these men were in their souls. As a middle-class kid who basically knew nothing about the world, the one thing I *did* know is that I wanted in. And not just for me. I wanted in for the both of us, big Joe and me. The man that was looking in from the outside. My dad.

I could only hope that someday, if I could play well enough to reach to the big leagues, he could sit with me, talk to my teammates, and share the joy he had given me all these years.

In September 1969, I reached the major leagues with the Los Angeles Dodgers. By mid-September we would visit Atlanta to play the Braves in a weekend series. On a Saturday about an hour before the game, the visiting clubhouse attendant came over to me and told me my dad was there. I remember going just outside the clubhouse and seeing Mom and Dad in the family waiting area. We hugged and I told Mom that Dad would be back in a few minutes. As we walked into the locker room Walter Alston—yes, the same skipper from my bat boy days—came out of the manager's office, saw us together, and said, "Hi Joe, the kid finally made it." Dad smiled, shook the skipper's hand, and said, "Thanks, Walt, he's worked hard." Dad turned around and we looked around the clubhouse. Dad caught me with those all-knowing eyes and said, "Your grandfather would have been proud, you made it." We'd all made it.

EPILOGUE

I hope you have enjoyed reading about my idols and the wonderful experiences I had as a young man growing up with them. Many of these men I would continue to see over the years. I even became one of them through my involvement in the game of baseball. The Boys of Summer aren't the only individuals who've taught me great life lessons. I've also had the opportunity to learn from teammates, opponents, other athletes (male and female), and business and religious leaders. Great and successful people live their lives for a reason. They live by certain parameters and have direction and motivation that define who they are and what they stand for, whether that thing is to please God, to seek material wealth, or to find out who one really is and what one can achieve. Successful people play what I call the "Game of Life." They invariably have a lineup and a strategy, they practice, and they keep score. Their wins and losses are noted and, ideally, learned from. Avoiding making the same mistake twice is important. Realizing and accepting that we are human beings and fallible is very important in the game. As in baseball, there's no time limit, and it's more of a marathon than a sprint. When you get knocked down, you have to get back up.

My personal philosophy is to live life with a winning lineup of virtues, supported by a bench full of motivation and execution skills, all for the glory of God and my family. To be perfectly honest, I have failed miserably at times during my life, but when I realized that we are on this earth to serve, I was able to get up each time and go to bat for what I believed in, wiser and stronger.

THE BOX SCORE FROM 1956

At St. Petersburg, Florida

Dodgers	AB.	H.	O.	A.	Yankees	AB.	H.	O.	A.
Neal, 2b	5	1	2	8	Lumpe, ss	5	2	2	7
Reese, ss	3	2	1	2	Bauer, lf	4	3	3	1
Zimmer, ss ...	1	0	0	2	Herzog, cf ...	5	0	0	0
Snider, cf	4	2	3	1	Berra, c	5	0	6	1
Hodges, 1b ...	3	1	7	0	Skoron, 1b ...	5	1	13	0
Williams, 1b ..	1	0	8	1	Collins, rf	2	1	1	0
Furillo, rf	5	2	0	0	Carey, 3b	5	2	1	8
J. Robinson, 1f	4	1	1	0	J. Coleman, 2b	4	1	4	2
Cimoli, 1f	1	0	0	0	Ford, p	1	0	0	0
Jackson, 3b ...	3	2	1	3	aE. Robinson .	1	0	0	0
Thompson, c .	1	0	2	1	Morgan, p	0	0	0	1
Howell, c	3	0	4	1	Freeman, p ...	1	0	0	0
Erskine, p	3	0	1	0	cThroneberry .	1	0	0	0
bAmoros	1	0	0	0	Konstanty, p ..	0	0	0	0
Labine, p	1	0	0	0	Totals	39	10	30	20
Totals	39	11	30	18					

Brooklyn Dodgers	4 0 0	0 0 0	0 0 0	1—5
New York Yankees	1 0 0	1 2 0	0 0 0	0—4

aStruck out for Ford in fifth.   bFlied out for Erskine in eighth.
cGrounded out for Freeman in ninth.   R—Reese, Hodges, Furillo,

J. Robinson, Cimoli, Bauer 2, Collins, Carey.   E—Carey, J. Coleman, Collins.   RBI—Hodges 2, Robinson 2, Bauer 2, J. Coleman, Lumpe.   2B—Furillo,   Snider,   Lumpe,   Jackson. HR—Hodges, Robinson, Bauer 2.   SH—Williams.   DP—Jackson, Neal, and Hodges; J. Coleman, Lumpe, and Skowron; Carey, J. Coleman, and Skowron.   LOB—Brooklyn 10, New York 9. BB—Erskine 1, Labine 3, Ford 2, Freeman 2.   SO—Ford 5, Freeman 1, Erskine 6.   Hits—Ford 7 in 5, Morgan 0 in 1, Freeman 2 in 3, Erskine 10 in 7.   R-ER—Ford 4-4, Erskine 4-4, Konstanty 1-0.   HP—Ford (Thompson).   WP—Freeman.   Winner—Labine. Loser—Konstanty.   U—Tabacchi (NL), Secory (NL), and Napp (AL).   T—2:51.   Attendance—8,468.

ACKNOWLEDGMENTS

This book has been a journey of love, commitment, and dedication, which could not have happened without the help of family, friends, and heroes.

To Candace, my wonderful wife, the love of my life. I thank you and love you for listening, over and over, to my "bat boy days" and for writing a treatment that is the heart and soul of this book. To Mom and Dad for giving me a life that made dreams come true. Thanks to my all-star literary agent Scott Waxman, who "got it" within the first few minutes of our first meeting to discuss this book. And to Brant Rumble and the team at Scribner, who do what they do better than anyone else, thanks for bringing this book to life. Ken Gurnick's hard work and collaboration have given all of us greater insight into America's baseball heroes.

And finally, I will always be indebted to the Boys of Summer, who taught so many of us how to be champions on and off the field and winners in life.